I0100478

INTELLECTUAL PROPERTY RIGHTS AND THEIR IMPORTANCE IN RESEARCH, BUSINESS AND INDUSTRY

The Editors

Dr. Ram Pratap Singh is currently working as Assistant Professor in Department of Botany, Govt. P.G. College, Morena (MP). Earlier, he served as Lecturer in Department of Botany, Institute of Basic Sciences, Bundelkhand University, Jhansi (UP). He obtained his M.Sc. and Ph.D degree from School of Studies in Botany, Jiwaji University, Gwalior (MP).

He was also awarded NET-JRF by (UGC-CSIR) in 2001. He has been teaching basic and advance Botany including Plant Taxonomy, Biotechnology and Plant Physiology at undergraduate and post graduate level for last ten years. Besides teaching, he is actively engaged in research activities. He is life time member of Indian Botanical Society and Indian Science Congress Association. He is edited a book on Biological Diversity and its Conservation by Daya Publishing House, New Delhi. He has published 12 research papers in National and international Journals of repute. He has organised several National Seminars.

Dr. Vinayak Singh Tomar did his post graduation in Zoology (1998) from Govt. Autonomous (Model) Science College, Gwalior (MP) and in Education (2004) from Govt. P.G. College of Education, Gwalior (M.P.). In 2003 completed his Ph.D. from Dr B.R. Ambedkar University, Agra. Dr. Tomar has been teaching graduate and post graduate classes for last 15th years. He has more than 20 research papers on his name which are published in various national and international journals, magazines and books.

He is life time member of many Zoological Research Organizations. He is the editor in chief of "Voyager" an international journal of science and life science and he also subject expert of various Government and Autonomous Colleges. He is also appointed as counselor in various Govt. institutions

Presently, he is working as Assistant Professor in the Department of Zoology, Govt. P. G. College of Excellence, Morena (MP).

INTELLECTUAL PROPERTY RIGHTS AND THEIR IMPORTANCE IN RESEARCH, BUSINESS AND INDUSTRY

–Editors–

DR. RAM PRATAP SINGH

Assistant Professor
Department of Botany
Govt. P. G. College, Morena (MP)

&

DR. VINAYAK SINGH TOMAR

Assistant Professor at CB
Department of Zoology
Govt. P. G. College, Morena (MP)

2014

Daya Publishing House®

A Division of

Astral International Pvt. Ltd.
New Delhi - 110 002

© 2014 EDITORS
ISBN 9789351302247

Publisher's note:
Every possible effort has been made to ensure that the information contained in this book is accurate at the time of going to press, and the publisher and author cannot accept responsibility for any errors or omissions, however caused. No responsibility for loss or damage occasioned to any person acting, or refraining from action, as a result of the material in this publication can be accepted by the editor, the publisher or the author. The Publisher is not associated with any product or vendor mentioned in the book. The contents of this work are intended to further general scientific research, understanding and discussion only. Readers should consult with a specialist where appropriate.
Every effort has been made to trace the owners of copyright material used in this book, if any. The author and the publisher will be grateful for any omission brought to their notice for acknowledgement in the future editions of the book.
All Rights reserved under International Copyright Conventions. No part of this publication may be reproduced, stored in a retrieval system, or transmitted in any form or by any means, electronic, mechanical, photocopying, recording or otherwise without the prior written consent of the publisher and the copyright owner.

Published by : **Daya Publishing House®**
A Division of
Astral International Pvt. Ltd.
– ISO 9001:2008 Certified Company –
4760-61/23, Ansari Road, Darya Ganj
New Delhi-110 002
Ph. 011-43549197, 23278134
E-mail: info@astralint.com
Website: www.astralint.com

Laser Typesetting : **Classic Computer Services**, Delhi - 110 035

Printed at : **Replika Press Pvt. Ltd.**

PRINTED IN INDIA

Dedicated to

our

RESPECTED TEACHERS

PREFACE

Intellectual property management encompasses creation, protection and exploitation of Intellectual Property Rights. Patents play a critical role in research and development of intensive industries. Patent rights are known to provide significant benefits as they can be sold or licensed and form foundation for making, using and selling industry leading products, processes and services. In order to obtain valid patent rights, however, basic knowledge of certain critical issues is considered essential among stakeholders.

We assessed the basic knowledge of proper record keeping practices, ownership and public disclosure among public and private sector organizations of various sizes across India and abroad in a variety of Industries. We found that respondents had good knowledge of proper record keeping practices assigning ownership of patents rights to the employers and excellent knowledge of what does not constitute a public disclosure and duration of the public disclosure grace period.

We recommended for implementing organizational processes for further educating stakeholders in obtaining valid patent rights for commercialization.

The explosive growth of digital technology advances significantly impacts the scope and nature of traditional intellectual property protection and management. It possess a new era of opportunity and challenges for national and international property protection.

This book deals with management and protection of intellectual property in present scenario.

We are extremely indebted to Dr. V. S. Tomar, Vice-chancellor JNKVV, Jabalpur (MP) for writing foreword for our book. We express our sincere thanks to him. We are also thankful to Dr. D. K. Bhatnagar, Principal, Govt. P. G. College, Morena (MP) for encouraging and guiding us.

We acknowledge our thanks to Daya Publishing House, New Delhi (A Division of Astral International Pvt. Ltd.) for publishing, this book in present format.

Book is focused on the scope of patents and related rights and gives reasons why patents and related rights need to be protected.

RAM PRATAP SINGH

VINAYAK SINGH TOMAR

प्रो. विजय सिंह तोमर
कुलपति

Prof. Vijay Singh Tomar
Vice-Chancellor

जवाहरलाल नेहरू कृषि विश्वविद्यालय
कृषि नगर, आधारताल, जबलपुर 482 004 म.प्र.
Jawaharlal Nehru Krishi Vishwa Vidyalaya
Krishi Nagar, Adhartal, Jabalpur
482 004 (M.P.)
No: - VC/TC/303,dt-27.11.2013

FOREWORD

Intellectual Property Right is the right of the people for their valuable creations. Intellectual Property Right (IPR) covers patent, copyright, trademark, industrial design, geographical indication, protection of layout design of integrated circuit and protection of plant variety.

Protection and exploitation of IPRs have provided significant benefits to both private and public sector organizations as these rights can be sold out or licensed to a buyer or licensor.

The exploitation of IPRs can add value by enhancing financial performance, establishing proprietary market, enhancing market share and producing high margins through greater competitiveness.

I understand that the present book entitled "*Intellectual Property Rights and their Importance in Research, Business and Industry*" will be of immense use for students, scholars, businessmen and teachers. Further, this book will also contribute in spreading awareness about Intellectual Property Rights and related issues.

I congratulate the authors and wish all the success.

(V.S. Tomar)

Ph.: 0761-2681706 (0), 2681809 (R); Fax:0761-2681389;E-mail:vstvcjnkw@gmail.com

CONTENT

LIST OF CONTRIBUTORS

AKHILESH CHANDRA RAGHUVANSHI,
> Department of Botany, S.M.S. Govt. Model Science College, Gwalior (MP)

A. K. UPADHYAY,
> Department of Physics, Govt. P.G. College, Morena (MP)

A. S. GAHLAUT
> Department of Chemistry, Govt. P.G. College, Morena (MP)

AMIT KUMAR SINGH CHAUHAN,
> Department of Botany, Govt. PG College, Morena (MP)

BASUKI NATH DUBEY,
> Mahatama Gandhi College of Law, Gwalior (MP)

BRAJESH KUMAR JATAV,
> Department of Botany, Govt. P. G. College, Datia (MP)

CHAITANYA KUMAR GOYAL,
> Department of Botany, Govt. P. G. College, Sheopur (M P)

D. B. RAI SHRIVASTAVA,
> Department of Mathematics, S. M. S. Govt. Model Science College, Gwalior (MP)

D. K. SHARMA,
> Department of Zoology, S. M. S. Govt. Model Science College, Gwalior (MP)

D. S. RATHORE,
> Department of Biotechnology, Govt. K.R.G. P.G. College, Gwalior (MP)

D. P. S. RATHORE,
> S. R. K. Inter College, Firozabad (UP)

DINESH K. CHATURVEDI,
> Department of Zoology, MJS Govt. PG College, Bhind (MP) Gwalior (MP)

ITI GONTIA-MISHRA,

Biotechnology Centre, Jawaharlal Nehru Agricultural University, Jabalpur (MP)

J. K. MISHRA ,

Department of Botany, Govt. P.G. College, Morena (MP)

K. S. SENGAR,

Govt. P. G. College, Sheopur (M P)

KESHAV S. JATAV,

Department of Botany, Govt. Chhatrasal College Pichhore, Shivpuri (MP)

KHUSHBOO BARDIYA - BHURAT, IPS

Academy, Indore (MP)

KRISHNAPAL SINGH CHAUHAN,

M. L. B. Arts and Commerce College, Gwalior, (M.P.)

MADHUP SHRIVASTAV,

School of Studies in Botany, Jiwaji University, Gwalior (MP)

MAMTA GUPTA,

Department of Botany, M.J.S. Govt. P.G. College, Bhind (MP)

MRIDUL PRATEEK SINGH,

National Law University, Vishakhapatnam (AP)

MUKULITA UPADHYAY,

Department of Zoology, Govt. P. G. College, Morena (MP)

N. K. BHARDWAJ,

Department of Physics, Govt. P.G. College, Morena (MP)

N. S. DADORIYA,,

Department of Environmental Science, Govt. P.G. College, Morena (MP)

NEERAJ BHARDWAJ,

Department of Military Science, Govt. College Alampur , Bhind (MP)

PAWAN AHIRWAR,

Department of Economics, Dr Hari Singh Gaur Central University, Sagar (MP)

PRAGYA SAXENA,

Department of Biotechnology, Govt. K.R.G. P.G. (Auto.) College, Gwalior (M.P.).

PRASHANT THOTE,

Gyanodaya Vidya Mandir, Narsingarh (MP)

PRATIBHA YADAR,

Holkar Science College, Indore,(M.P)

PRERNA MITRA,

Department of Botany, Govt. P G College, Mandsaur (MP)

R.K. GARG,

Centre of Excellence in Biotechnology, MPCST, Bhopal (M.P.)

R. L. SAKHAWAR,,

Department of Botany, Govt. P.G. College, Morena (MP)

R. P. SINGH,

Department of Botany, Govt. P. G. College, Morena (MP)

RAJDEEP KUDESIA,

Department of Botany, Bundelkhand University, Jhansi (UP)

RAJENDRA SINGH RATHORE,

Department of Botany, Govt. M.J.S. P.G. College, Bhind (M.P.)

RAM KHILARI,

Ministry of Science & Technology, Department of Scientific & Industrial Research (DSIR), New Delhi

RAMAVTAR SHARMA,

Department of Military Science, Govt. Science College ,Gwalior (MP)

RENU SINGH,

Department of Political Science Govt. Girls College, Bhind (MP)

S. S. NIGAM,

Department of Chemistry, Govt. P G College, Morena (MP)

S. P. SHARMA,

Department of Economics, Govt. P. G. College, Morena (MP)

SADHANA DIXIT,

Department of Hindi, Govt. P G College, Morena (MP)

SADHNA PANDEY,

Department of Botany, Govt. K.R.G. P.G. College, Gwalior (MP)

SARITA SHRIVASTAVA,

Department of Zoology, Govt. Model Science College, Gwalior (MP)

SAROJ SHRIVASTAVA,

Department of Economics, Sarojini Naidu Govt. Girls P. G. College, Bhopal (MP)

SHOBHITA UPADHYAY,

Department of English, Govt. Model Science College, Gwalior (MP)

SUBHASH CHAND,

Department of Botany, Govt. P. G. College, Sheopur (M P)

SUDHIR KUMAR PATHAK,

Department of Botany, Govt. M. J. S. P. G. College, Bhind (M.P.)

V. S. MTSANIYA,

Department of Economics, Dr. Hari Singh Gaur Central University, Sagar (MP)

VINAYAK SINGH TOMAR,

Department of Zoology, Govt. P. G. College, Morena (MP)

Chapter-1

ENHANCING COMPETITIVENESS OF SMEs THROUGH TECHNOLOGY MANAGEMENT: PERSPECTIVES AND PROSPECTS

RAM KHILARI

Ministry of Science & Technology,
Department of Scientific & Industrial Research (DSIR), New Delhi

Globalization coupled with liberalization and privatization has posed serious threats and challenges to SMEs to remain sustainable, at the same time it has created vast opportunities to them to become competitive in the Global Markets. After WTO regime, the global economy, characterized with open markets and free trade policies has intensified competition and constant pressure to the emerging economies leading to the emergence of competitiveness as an important indicator for economic development. The new open market economy has thus posed threats to the nations, more particularly to the developing and least developing ones, to realize and put emphasis on improving performance of SMEs, produce quality products and capture sophisticated markets. It is a fact that the SMEs are significantly contributing to the respective national economies, employment generation and mitigation of social problems like health, hunger and poverty. But the basic feature of development of SMEs has been to function and perform on old age/obsolete technology, poor quality of products and restricted markets. The nations, have now realized the need to collaborate and compete. This has necessitated developing core competencies by SMEs in their respective areas of operations. The slackdown in the economic growth in the late 90's and mounting business failures across several industrial sectors brought the issue of competitiveness to the forefront in India. Many industrial sectors in India have faced the surviving crisis and most sufferers in this process have been the SME sector.

---

* Views expressed in this paper are of the author, and do not necessarily reflect the views of the Department.

The SME competitiveness can be enhanced at country level, corporate level and firm/industry level. It is in this context the role of Technology Management becomes more important and necessary in enhancing SME competitiveness at all levels not for India, but for all developing and least developing countries. An effort has been made in this chapter to discuss and understand the dynamics of competitiveness, concepts of Technology Management and its Need for SMEs, and a set of recommendations/suggestions for enhancing SME competitiveness through Technology Management are made.

2. Competitiveness and Its Importance to SMEs

Competitiveness has relevance at different levels and achieving global competitiveness at any level often requires synergistic linkages with other levels. Macroeconomic environments at the industry and country levels play crucial role in shaping competitiveness of firms and industries. Understanding linkages among different levels is essential for enhancing competitiveness at any level.

Competitiveness can be defined at three levels: nation, industry/sector and company. The functional definitions of competitiveness in its most abstracted form at three levels relevant for our purpose are given below:

- **Country Competitiveness:** Extent to which a national environment is conducive or detrimental to business.

- **Industry/Sector Competitiveness:** Extent to which an industry or a business sector offers potential for growth and attractive return on investment. The concept can also be defined as the collective ability of firms in the sector to compete internationally.

- **Company Competitiveness:** Ability to design, produce and/or market products or services superior to those offered by competitors, considering the price and non-price qualities.

The terms industry and sector are technically different, but can be considered equivalent and are used interchangeably. **A more performance-oriented definition of industry competitiveness can be given as: Collective ability of an industry on performance factors such as productivity, cost, market share, international share and technology.**

Competition is a necessity in today's world order. One needs to be competitive to succeed against competition. Competitiveness is a foundation for the success of any company or industry or country. It is a concept that has long-term implications for the industries and is the initial point of strategic thinking for the organizations. The success or failure of a company depends on the extent of competitive advantage it enjoys vis-à-vis its rivals in delivering the quality product/service to the customer at lower cost. Organisations need to learn about creation and sustenance of competitive advantages in their respective segments.

Competitiveness shapes survival and success of strategic policies of a nation in today's globally competitive business environment. The competitive firms/industries are having better chances for their survival, whereas non-competitive firms may disappear from the scene. Thus there is a positive co-relation between economic development and competitiveness of a country, and competitiveness has emerged as an important indicator for all round development of a country. The concept, therefore, has now got wider recognition, appreciation and due attention in India.

To improve industrial competitiveness of any industry or enterprise, it is most important to understand and evaluate objectively the performance of these industries/ enterprises so that their weaknesses may be identified and ways and means to improve it may be explored.

3. Technology Management for Small & Medium Enterprises

The SME sector in India is blessed with a number of challenges and variety of complexities. The industries which have been able to restructure their resources management practices for optimal utilization in terms of infrastructure, technology, product diversification, better marketing strategies, and finances, etc. have been successful to retain their competitive position both in the domestic as well as in the global markets. On the other hand, many of them which have not been able to organize their efforts in the right direction and did not change with the changing situations have either gone sick or are closed. Evidently, the technology has played an important role in shaping the wellbeingness of the SMEs. The technology management, therefore, as a function will play an increasing role in enhancing competitiveness of the SMEs. For that reason, it is necessary to understand technology management process and its dynamics for addressing issues being faced by the industry.

What is Technology Management?

It may be defined as ability to manage all aspects of technology starting from concept to the commercialization i.e. access to information related to technologies, sources of technology, generation of technology, commercialization and competitiveness, etc.

Why Technology Management for SMEs?

Nations world over have realized that having access to or possessing the excellent technology in itself does not enable one to compete successfully. Globally, several phenomena have been taking place: innovation has gained focus, research has become of far greater consequence, technology life cycles have become much shorter, products have considerable variety and far shorter life spans, new product development has become paramount, rapid generation and commercialization of new technologies has become necessary.

Moreover, critical technologies are not readily available from any source. Research programmes are not only very intensive but also very risky; and collaboration in research has been the pragmatic solution in some cases. Many countries are opting to establish research bases in other countries. Some kinds of technology development are of such a large magnitude that resources of any single nation in terms of finance or manpower are not sufficient to deal with the situation.

At the organizational level, technology is intertwined with every function, be it marketing or finance or services, not only manufacturing or research. Besides, intellectual property rights have gained immense significance and it has become crucial to understand and handle the various intricacies associated with these property rights and the intangible wealth linked to the technology one deals with.

The SMEs with meager financial resources, lack of skills and management capabilities, and changing market dynamics are not able to concentrate on technology development and its upgradation. Though R&D is an important component to continuously upgrade knowledge and technology, but it requires large investment and hence is beyond the reach of SMEs. They are facing tough competition, both at domestic as well as at international level because of large number MNCs are either dumping their products in the Indian markets or are coming with latest technologies. The gap between the development of new products and its commercialization is so short that for SMEs it becomes very difficult to meet the consumer requirements in a time-bound manner. Equally important challenges to SMEs are to cope and adjust with the national policies of development which emphasizes use of energy-efficient and environment-friendly technologies.

The technological process alone is not sufficient to combat challenges effectively in the current competitive environment; rather the ability to manage these skills is equally important. Technology management is the key to performance in every sphere of activity in the current milieu; be it finance or marketing or manufacturing or services. In this context, there is a need to understand both business and technology, and the ability to manage the various aspects of technology.

Major Issues in Technology Management for SMEs

The process of management of technology is very complex in nature. It encompasses so many issues. Over the years, the subject has got wider appreciation and recognition at all levels including academic circles, R&D organizations, corporate, firms/industries and service organizations at national, regional and organizational levels. A few years back, the Department of Scientific & Industrial Research (DSIR), Govt. of India, visualized some of the key issues pertaining to management of technology, which are depicted below:

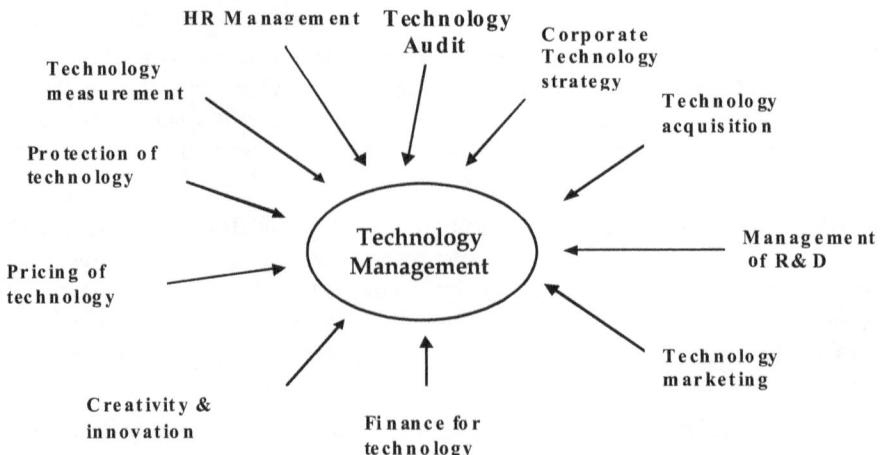

These individual entities in the depiction can have important impact on the commercial performance of firms/industry or organization in the short term or even in the long term. It is very important and desirable to give a thrust equally to manage these individual entities in an integrated manner to maximise benefits at the desired levels.

The management of technology transfer and acquisition is a issue of concern to all. This is because it is being increasingly realized that merely the purchasing or development of suitable technology, or mere possession of excellent technology, would really be of no avail. The realization is that excellent technology can reap no results, unless effective measures are continuously taken to implement the technology so as to sustain ultimate product quality, with commensurate cost incompliance with varied customer preference. This means that a systematic manner of dealing with the issues concerned involving the entire process, or, put differently, proper overall management, is a must. The proper management of technology acquisition, covers a host aspects from decisions concerning acquisition, as against development of technology, the specific components of technology to be procured, the forms and channels for acquisition, the appropriate timing for acquisition, scanning the relevant sources for technology, selection of suitable technology sources, evaluation of technology, negotiating, concerns regarding intellectual property rights, drawing up the agreement keeping in view all legal formalities and technological requirements, preparing for the implementation, providing for training, suitable steps for absorption, assimilation and further upgradation of the inducted technology and more.

The need to have an appropriate technology strategy is stressed upon. That drawing up a technology strategy involves a total preparedness for facing the onslaught of technological changes, which are inevitable and perpetual and this preparedness can be organized - at the entrepreneurial level, at the business unit level, at the organizational level and at the national level - through suitable preparation, planning, organizing, execution, implementation, monitoring and administering on a continuing, on-going basis. That a suitable strategy can only be drawn if a structured information basis exists in each and every entity managing technology. Also, very importantly that a strategy for technology needs to be in complete fusion with the business strategy. That the entire process of technology acquisition and development needs to be orchestrated so as to increase the technology base of the entity concerned as that alone would lead it towards development of core competencies, self sufficiency, technological strength and the ultimate goal of competitiveness.

Technology Audit is a systematic approach to assess the technological strengths and weaknesses of the organization/industry against the most relevant competitor. Its focus is on core competencies of a technological unit. Technology Audit is an integral component of formulation of technology strategy for a company. Likewise technology benchmarking is also an important aspect of Technology Management and may be carried out by SMEs to sustain their technological competitive position.

Protection of technology so generated is more vital. In the days ahead each firm/industry would have to depend on the strength of its technology base as the knowledge resident in the technology base is ultimately going to be responsible for retaining existing core competencies and for development of new competencies. In view of the impending changes in the international trade rules and regulations, the need to foster great care and attention to the management of creativity and innovation in any enterprise is very important. An understanding of these issues and their relationship with intellectual property rights covering a gamut of aspects including their implication in technology transfer and acquisition are covered.

The pricing of technology has many complexities associated with it. The appropriate costing of development efforts, in many cases over extended periods of time, is just one of the expected sales of the product/products generated as an outcome of the technology, the expected profits to be generated by the parties in a deal, the expected capital infrastructure for different scales of production, the expected range of technology licensing, the effect of licensing on internal development in monetary terms and the expectation of the ultimate consumer.

The proper management of research and development in this environment is of prime importance, and need to be given due emphasis. Selection of suitable projects, structured methods for their implementation, measures for effective monitoring of their progress, systems for financing the projects in an organization and other related aspects are very important. Both large national research and development laboratories as well as academic institutes need to effectively manage the entire process to suit their individual organizational cultures. So also industry organization need to develop a suitable culture for the fostering of innovation. That this can help the entities concerned reap very large rewards over extended periods of time through appropriate management.

Marketing of technology another complex issue. Whether a technology push strategy or a technology pull strategy is involved, it is being realized that the ultimate consumer should be convinced over a sufficiently long period of time and kept satisfied. Any enterprise needs to rapidly reposition itself for extreme competitive preparedness and ensure a successful transition from an area of regulation and protection that existed in the country till 1991, to the fully globalized market that exists today. This competitiveness that empower them to adapt quickly to changing opportunities, which is the only changing reality of the future.

Suitable techniques for the measurement of various indices used in the process of managing technology and the modality of implementing procedures such as technology forecasting are also important.

The Management of Human Resources and Intellectual Property right is another vital component of Technology Management, without proper human resource management talking of Technology Management and Competitiveness is of no avail. The firms should devise methods and formulate mechanism to induct "right people with right skills for right jobs, and strive for their capacity building by enhancing skills and knowledge and opening opportunities for increasing their potential to work and innovate. The industry should be well aware about the issues of IPR and its management so that the innovation created in the company/industry is protected.

4.   Suggestions/recommendations for Enhancing Industrial Competitiveness through Technology Management

It is mandatory to catalyze national efforts in developing technology management capabilities by providing technical inputs and support mechanisms including developing tools and techniques for efficient transfer and management of technology. Specific programmes targeted towards enhancing technology management capability building in industry, R&D and consultancy organizations, academic institutes and other establishments need to be initiated.

Suggested Activities

The following activities may beneficial:

- Enhancing knowledge base in respect of technologies specific to the nation, including rural based technologies and region/sector specific technologies by undertaking analytical studies, technology status and development studies;

- Providing information to industry, Government departments, researchers through targeted research studies and policy research;

- Promoting industry-institute interaction by setting up resource centers on technology management in appropriate locations;

- Curriculum development exercises;

- Enhancing academic interest and contribution through active collaborations and memorandums of understanding with academic institutes;

- Providing assistance in efficient transfer of technology, through information in respect of foreign collaborations approved and analysis of such approvals as well as focused studies;

- Initiating state level agencies and research organizations to take up activities in the realm of Technology Management;

- Information dissemination on Technology Management related aspects through newsletters, manuals, and other forms

- Promoting an understanding of Technology Management in the Indian scenario through case studies of manufacturing and research organizations in the country, etc.

- Conducting awareness programmes, focused training courses, seminars and management development programmes, and providing guidance to trainers.

A few important activities are discussed below:

Analytical, Technology Status and Development Studies

There has been need for studies covering sector-specific status of technology in the country, international trends, gaps in technology, research facilities and other such information; in respect of specific identified products, processes. There are also a number of areas where there is need for indigenous development of technology and for value addition, including rural based technologies, in respect of which information collection and analysis is required. Also, there are many region specific resources in different States in the country that have spawned industries, which could benefit through further research and analysis in respect of value addition, technology upgradation and information dissemination. Identification of technology gaps in existing industries in respect of important products and processes is an important requirement that needs to be continually addressed. Industry, policy makers, consultants, academic and research institutes are provided with implementation in areas of their concern relating to technologies in which effective action can be taken to mitigate problems and enhance efficiency.

Studies on technology and innovation management issues

Technological dynamism has become the order of the day and new approaches; tools and techniques are being developed in technology and innovation management areas. Specific studies - in such emerging areas for harnessing value from knowledge leading to further knowledge creation, on technology transfer issues and technology up-gradation measures, and   in other technology areas for the benefit of small and medium enterprises need to be taken up. Identified sectors that offer opportunity for growth of SMEs may be prioritized for these studies.

Targeted research studies on specific issues in technology transfer, technology and innovation management

There is need for serious research and study of several aspects concerned with management of technology in different sectors that are important for the economic uplift of the nation. This is to develop an objective understanding of complex situations demanding a focused direction. Such research efforts will not only result in comprehensive information and data collection of a specific nature but also enable analytical decision making capability.

Case Studies covering Technology Management aspects

The objective is to generate learning from best practices and to study and analyze the manner in which technology is managed in Indian enterprises. Apart from being useful for pedagogic use, these case studies will provide useful information to consultants and executives from industry.

Collaborative work with Academic and Research Institutes:

In order to give the necessary thrust to formal education and develop a base of teaching tools on technology management aspects, the collaborative work with academic institutes, especially those concerned with technical and management education need to be taken up seriously. Different activities, inclusive of management development programmes and projects on technology and innovation management in association with different institutions may be commonly worked out.

Technology & Innovation Management Centres (TIMCs)

Centres for Technology and Innovation Management need to be set up in different locations of the country where there is access to information on aspects concerned with the subject that are of specific interest to the region of concern, expertise to advise and provide guidance on issues concerned with technology management, and generate long-term as well as short-term solutions. The activities to be taken up by these centres may include : training, research, cluster development studies, case studies, scouting innovation, manpower development, interfacing between academia and industries, data generation, sharing of knowledge and providing solutions to industries, preparation of technology related policy studies, developing training tools and modules.

Creation of Technology Management Chairs

Providing assistance to institutions in respect of education in technology management has been one of the focus areas of the Technology Management . There is a need to initiate creation of TM chairs in small institutes with clusters of industries where there is large concentration of SMEs.

Training/Interaction meets/Seminars/Management Development Programmes

The major focus of these programmes is capacity building in the area of Technology Management by creating awareness, providing training, organizing management development programmes, etc. for the benefit of SMEs.

In summing up is recommended

(i)   There is a need to create greater awareness amongst the SMEs about the issues of competitiveness and technology management at all levels.

(ii)   There is a need to organize capacity building programmes in specific components of technology management particularly for SMEs by way of conducting short-term as well as long-term training, workshops/seminars and EDPs/MDPs.

(iii)   More Technology and Innovation Management Centres may be set up in the areas where there is a large concentration of SME clusters so that the Centres can address issues and needs being faced by SMEs in a particular region of concern.

(iv)   For creation of knowledge and research beneficial to the SMEs and Rural industries, there is a need to create Technology Management Chairs in smaller institutions in remote parts of the country.

(v)   SMEs may emphasize and work more rigorously on integration of their technology strategies with business strategies.

(vi)   SMEs may strive to do more R&D and innovation on processes, products and services and continuously upgrade knowledge and technology.

(vii)   For easy access to information on technology, innovation, products and markets, SMEs may use more and more IT tools effectively.

(viii) There is a need to develop collaborations and networking with academic institutes, R&D organizations, Management Institutes and Associations of

SMEs so that effective measures can be taken for generating knowledge, tools and techniques for managing technology and innovation and enhancing competitiveness.

(ix)   The SMEs may put major thrust on quality products and for that the quality management practices such lean manufacturing practices, etc. may be adopted.

REFERENCES

1.   Report on Competitiveness in Emerging Industries - An Exploratory Study by IIT, Delhi: Department of Scientific & Industrial Research (DSIR), New Delhi, 2007.

2.   Kiran Momaya; International Competitiveness - Evaluation and Enhancement, 2001.

3.   Vinay Kumar & Jyoti S.A. Bhat: Dynamics of Managing Technology in a Growing Economy - A National Perspective: Case of India - TCDPAP Training Programme on "Issues in Technology Management for Small & Medium Enterprises" - Hanoi, Vietnam 27-28 February, 2006.

4.   Guidelines - Technology Management Programme (TMP): Department of Scientific & Industrial Research (DSIR), New Delhi; December 2005.

Chapter-2

INTELLECTUAL PROPERTY RIGHTS IN EDUCATION: AN ANALYSIS OF TEACHERS AWARENESS IN CENTRAL INDIA

PRASHANT THOTE & D. P. S. RATHORE*
Gyanodaya Vidya Mandir, Narsingarh (MP)
*S. R. K. Inter College, Firozabad (UP)

The present study is an attempt to find the awareness on Intellectual Property Right in Education among secondary school teachers of Damoh District, Central India. The information was gathered through a questionnaire constructed for this purpose. The questionnaire consists of 40 questions related to awareness on Intellectual Property Right. A survey was conducted among 200 respondents by using the questionnaire. The data collected were grouped and analyzed using mean, SD 't' test. Findings revealed that the secondary school teachers of Damoh district have significant awareness on Right to Education Act. The result of the survey showed that the Intellectual Property Right awareness must still be more promoted.

INTRODUCTION

The concept of intellectual property (IP) will be understood better if we understand what is meant by the term property. To a lay mind, property means some material object belonging to a particular person. The concept of ownership is critical to the concept of property. Ownership means the right to possess, use and dispose the property at the desire of the owner, to exclude the others. If a society does not recognize ownership, it will not have a concept of property. In the legal sense, property refers to the bundle of rights that the law confers on a person by virtue of the ownership and possession of an object. However, a material object under one's possession may not amount to much as property if it does not become a resource to satisfy some human want or need. By exertion of his intellect, either in the form of ideas or technology, man converts a natural resource into something of utility, making it an item of property. The first is scarcity, which refers to its availability in relation to the need. The scarcer is a thing in relation to the demand for it, the higher is its value. The second important factor influencing the value of an object is the knowledge of its use or uses. The higher the value of an object, the more zealously it is guarded as a property. You may ask, what rights constitute the bundle of rights that are termed as property?

These rights deal with various aspects of the relationship between man and his property, such as: ownership and possession; use and enjoyment of the fruits of the application of property; exclusion of others from use and application of the property; and transfer of rights in the property. The property can relate to a tangible thing e.g. land or buildings, or to an intangible thing e.g. a copyright. In the former case they are referred to as corporeal property, in the latter case they are known as incorporeal property corporeal property has a big advantage over incorporeal property. The fact of possession of a physical object by the owner ensures that any other person is excluded from using it. It is not so with the creations of the mind, say, an invention or a book which can b reproduced without authorization. With the advances in technology, newer means of copying have become available, mass copying has become easy and the cost of reproduction has come down. This brings us to the concept of intellectual property. It is simply the property created by the application of human mind. It is non-physical (incorporeal) and it derives its value from idea(s). There is no uniform definition of IP. The domain of IP is expanding fast as knowledge and information becomes key driver of echo-economic growth and of societal progress in general. IP is a dynamic area. As science and technology make rapid advances and as competition for markets becomes ever fiercer, human ingenuity is throwing up ever new ideas and newer products. Different types of IP rights like patent, copyright, trade mark, design etc. can protect these ideas and products. Newer areas are emerging with claims for recognition as IP. They have to be accommodated as IP either in one of the existing categories or in new categories that have to be created. For example, copyright originally was concerned with works of literature and art, gradually its scope expanded to cover works of drama, music, photography, cinematography, audio-visual recordings, performances, broadcasts and now computer programmes. It is recognized that the term copyright cannot justifiably applied to all these creations: therefore, the category of related rights or neighboring right had to be introduced. As school teachers are important and role model in the society awareness programmer in India may b successful if proper awareness programmer may be implemented. Hence to know the ground zero reality present study is index taken by the authors.

The importance of Copyright education and promotional activities must be clearly announced in India. To implement copyright education and awareness building activities, it is effective and crucial to do so in the formal School Education. Learning the impact of digitization for everyday life and society, think about the importance of

Information moral. Teach the protection of privacy and copyright as well as the responsibility of sending information through the example of the Internet. Moral in the highly developed Information Communication Society-teach the attitude in personal or business life to live independently in the information society, protection of privacy and copyright, responsibility of sending information and management of information security.

The State shall take the necessary measures to promote education and learning on intellectual Property and provide knowledge on intellectual property through public relations activities, etc. in order to develop a society in which intellectual property rights are respected, through making the public more aware f and deepening its interest in intellectual property.

DEVELOPING HUMAN RESOURCES AND IMPROVING PUBLIC AWARENESS

Training instructors specializing in intellectual property: With growing demand for human resources related to .intellectual property in various fields, including elementary/secondary educational institutions and universities as well as private companies, this will continue to actively provide information on the study of the latest practical educational programs and the results of such study, and train instructors and teachers through intensive training programs.

Promoting intellectual property education at schools: The schools will continue to promote intellectual property education according to the respective school levels, such as considering the enhancement of educational activities that cultivate children's creativity upon revising the ministry's curriculum guideline.

Strengthening activities for improving public awareness of intellectual property: The school will continue to hold seminars on intellectual property for students, adults in general, and practitioners based on their respective attributes, by also making use of intellectual property specialists in the private sector, and promote active use of such seminars according to the circumstances of the respective communities. The institute will also enhance awareness-raising projects such as a campaign using a publicly solicited slogan.

Copyright Education in Schools: To implement copyright education and awareness building activities, it is effective and crucial to do so in the formal School Education. In the Indian education system, every school from kindergarten to high school has to obey the curriculum. Learning the impact of digitization for everyday life and society, think about the importance of Information (moral teach) the protection of privacy and copyright as well as the responsibility of sending information through the example of the Internet. Moral in the highly developed Information Communication Society teach the attitude in personal or business life to live independently in the information society, protection of privacy and copyright, responsibility of sending information and management of information security.

For Students: Creates and distributes Computer Aided Instruction System or Edutainment software on copyright protection. They can be accessed at the web site publishes a cartoon pamphlet. It is distributed to all students of fifteen years old.

For School Teachers: Higher Educational Institute hold Copyright Seminars for teachers. It is held once a year and transmitted via video-net. A pamphlet "Educational activities in schools and copyright" explains the limitations and exceptions on copyright and related rights concerning school activities another pamphlet." How to use 5 minutes for copyright education?" makes it possible for teachers to teach copyright system in every subject's lesson using fragmental times.

Activities for General Public and Specialists: Outside schools, JCO holds a variety of copyright workshop programs for librarians, teachers, and officials of local government in charge of copy right as well as for the general public. JCO is also building a Virtual Copyright Help Desk, which aims to handle inquiries from these people on the JCO website. Number of leaflets on various issues and topics targeted for instance, beginners, specialists, teachers, librarians and children, are produced and distributed for free to educational institutions, prefecture or municipal bodies, publics firms, etc. as well as anyone interested in copyright. CRIC produce cartoon pamphlet as well as JCO. They distribute it to all pupils of nine years old. CRIC creates a series of Video Programmes and provide rending service for free for schools and other meetings to learn copyright. It includes a programmes of quiz show on Copyright, a program targeted teenager featuring TV star and a programmes for children using famous animation character.

At the conclusion, I would like to summarize the copyright awareness raising and training in India.

1. Importance of awareness building activities is clearly defined by national policy.

2. Activities are implemented by both of Government, India Copyright Office and private sector CRIC side by side.

3. Private organization plays important role in the Awareness Raising activities.

Objectives of the study

The following objectives are preferred to conduct this study

1. To find out the level of awareness on RTE among Secondary School teachers of Central India

2. To find out the significant difference if any between the different groups of demographic variables such as -sex, teacher's residence, location of school, types and nature of school in awareness on IPR in Education.

3. To give suggestions to improve the level of awareness on IPR in Education among Secondary School Teachers.

Hypotheses

1. The level of awareness on IPR in Education among Secondary School teachers is very low.

2. There is a significant difference between the different groups of sex. Student residence and location of school, types and nature of school in awareness on IPR in Education among Secondary school teachers of Damoh District.

3. Secondary school teachers who are residing in rural area have more awareness on IPR in Education.

4. Female teachers a have more awareness on IPR in Education.

METHODOLOGY

Research design: The investigator preferred normative survey method to collect data from the Secondary school teachers. The investigator employed simple random sampling technique in order to collect data from the students studying at secondary level.

Population: The Population of the present study comprised of all the Secondary School Teachers working in Damoh district affiliated to M.P. Board and CBSE.

Sample: From the total population of secondary school teachers in different schools f Damoh. Sample of 200 teachers has been taken.

Tool: A self prepared questionnaire which contains 60 questions dealing with understanding, application and knowledge about IPR in education. Out of 60 questions, 12 questions is based on the rating scale, 20 right wrong types and rest is on multiple choices.

Statistical techniques: Mean Standard Deviation and t-Test.

Table -1: Showing the awareness of IPR among Secondary School Teachers (N=200)

Score	Frequency	Percentage	Category
30-40	120	60	Low awareness
40-50	40	20	Poor
50-60	20	10	Below average
60-70	30	15	Average
70-80	10	05	Above average
80-90	00	00	Good
90-100	00	00	High awareness
Total	200	10	

Mean 68.38   SD 7.85

Table -2: Differences in the Level of IPR Awareness among the Teachers

Variables		N	Mean	SD 6.89	T Value	Level of Significance
Age	Below 35	99	66	8.4	3.53	Not Significant
	Above 35	101	63	5.96		
Educational Qualification.	M.Sc.	100	65	7.88	1.39	Not Significant
	M.A.	100	65	6.56		
Professional Qualification	B.Ed.	180	67	5.59	1.35	Not Significant
	M.Ed.	20	64	7.65		
Gender	Male	65	66	7.85	0.78	Not Significant
	Female	135	64	7.83		
Marital status	Unmarried	50	68	7.25	0.04	Not Significant
	Married	150	67	7.66		
Area of residence	Rural	100	65	7.65	0.05	Not Significant
	Urban	100	66	8.6		
School affiliation	M.P.Board	110	67	8.33	1.86	Not Significant
	C.B.S.E.	90	68	9.65		
Type of school	Government	50	69	6.76	1.65	Not Significant
	Private	150	68	7.98		
Medium of instructions	English	100	68	8.4	1.78	Not Significant
	Hindi	100	65	7.66		
Type of family	Nuclear	160	66	8.59	3.65	Not Significant
	Joint	40	67	8.56		
Reading habit-	Regularly	40	66	6.85	3.45	Significant
(News Papers/Circulars	Rarely	160	68	6.25		

Table -3 Analysis of choice of training by school teachers on IPR

Type of training	First Choice		Second Choice		Third Choice	
	N	%	N	%	N	%
Workshop	108	54	56	28	52	26
Literature	60	30	104	54	40	20
One to one	20	10	28	14	32	16
Peer Group	12	06	08	04	68	32

RESULTS AND DISCUSSIONS

Table -1 show that 60% of schools teacher belong to "Low Awareness" Category which indicate that 30% school teachers do not have any awareness of IPR. Further 20% teachers belong to category of the "poor awareness" which means they have a little bit knowledge about the IPR 10% of the teacher's com in the category of the

"Below Average" which means, they have some awareness about IPR. Next is "average "category" which contains 15% teachers, it indicates that these 05% teachers are "Above average". None has a "Good Knowledge" and "high awareness" level. From analysis, out of these 100 scores, the mean score comes out 68.38 in case of school teachers which are very close to the average scores.

Table -2: shows that there exists no significant difference in the awareness level educational qualification, professional qualification, and male and female, unmarried and married, rural and urban, M.P. and C.B.S.E. Affiliated Government and private English and Hindi, Nuclear and joint family at both 0.01 and 0.05 level of significant difference. There is significant difference between the awareness level among the teacher who has age below 35 and above 35. The awareness of young teacher is more than older teachers.

There is significant difference between the teachers having regular reading habit and rarely reading habit. Teachers having regular reading habit high awareness towards IPR.

It is inferred from Table -3 that most of teacher's first choice was workshop followed by per discussion and provide them literature.

CONCLUSION

- The study reveals that there is a low level of awareness about IPR act among Primary School Teachers in Central India.

- The awareness level among male and female teachers is quite equal.

- There is no significant difference between married and unmarried teachers regarding IPR.

- The right to education act awareness level in science and art post graduate teachers is quite equal.

- The awareness level in B.Ed. and M.Ed. teachers is quite equal.

- Urban and rural primary school teachers have same level of awareness towards IPR.

- Teacher teaching M.P. Board and C.B.S.E. has equal awareness.

- Teachers teaching in Hindi and English medium school have quite equal awareness.

- Teachers having joint family having higher awareness level than unclear family IPR.

- Teachers having regular reading habit having higher awareness level towards IPR.

Limitations of the study

After respective view of the whole study, the investigators find that there were a few limitations that constricted the area of generalization of this study. The limitations were as given below:

1. Due to paucity of time and resources a sample of only 100 primary school teachers was taken which restricted the scope of generalization.

2. There are many variables which may affect the awareness of teachers towards IPR like some socio-economic variables, intellectual level, and maturity level and so on. Though these variables were included in the study, they were not used in analysis in any way.

3. Since the awareness was measured on the basis of fixed responses, the students might have given socially accepted responses instead of giving correct responses.

4. Only a very few schools affiliated to CBSE and MP board were selected in this study.

5. Some respondents put tick mark against more than one alternative and sometimes they left some of the items unanswered which presented difficulty in accurate analysis of data.

6. The biggest limitation was that some teachers consulted with each other while making their choice. So the result might have got affected due to this.

7. Present study was conducted only in one state therefore more empirical evidences will be required from more states before sufficient generalization may be made. In light of this, it is suggested that a similar but more elaborate study may be conducted using a larger sample and covering more states in India.

Recommendations

(1) A workshop and seminars should be conducted at school level to improve the awareness

(2) Literature should be provided preferable in the mother tongue so that they may read and understand the IPR creaky

REFERENCES

1. Study material Indira Gandhi National Open University, New Delhi.

Chapter-3

PATENTS IN BIOTECHNOLOGY: DEVELOPMENT, CONTROVERSIES AND SOCIAL CONSIDERATIONS

ITI GONTIA-MISHRA[1] and KHUSHBOO BARDIYA - BHURAT[2]

[1]*Biotechnology Centre, Jawaharlal Nehru Agricultural University, Jabalpur (MP).*
[2]*IPS Academy, Indore (MP).*

Biotechnology is the result of intellectual labour; it is an application of human ingenuity to biological processes. It involves human interference to a biological process. Human intervention differentiates biotechnological process from biological process. Naturally biological process takes place without human intervention. When there is human intervention to this biological process, it results in producing new things previously not in existence. This effort of intellectual labour deserves protection under patent law. These non-naturally occurring, human made and synthetically produced inventions of biotechnology shall be protected to get the desired fruits and also to encourage further research and development. 'A patent gives an inventor a period of exclusive exploitation (up to 20 years in the UK) in return for a disclosure of the invention' (Huskisson, 1996).

The main aim and object of this review is to highlight and explore the inter-relationship of an intellectual property right with the biotechnological inventions and to focus on its related controversies and social concerns.

What is Biotechnology?

Biotechnology is broadly defined as any technique that uses living organisms to make or modify products, to improve plants or animals, or to develop microorganisms for specific uses. Biotechnology is not a single technique but a collection of techniques utilized to manipulate living organisms in directed fashions. The development of biotechnology has removed the initial barrier between biology and technology. By its very nature, biotechnology when utilised towards practical application is multidisciplinary, requiring team approach directed at targeted goals. A series of advanced technologies spanning biology, chemistry, biochemistry, microbiology, protein engineering, process engineering and genetic engineering put together and collectively called as biotechnology. The two significant factors, which lie at the base of India's biotechnology potential, are the scientific and technical pool of human resources and secondly the rich biodiversity of the country, hence it could be exploited for patenting technologies (Kumar and Das, 2010). Since research and development in biotechnology is extremely time consuming and requires huge investment, granting Intellectual Property Rights (IPR) is an effective tool to protect biotechnology inventions (Graff et al., 2002).

Applications and Scopes of Biotechnology

Historically speaking, biotechnology was an art in the production of wines, beers, cheese through fermentation process. Presently, biotechnology comprises of modern techniques such as DNA technology and genetic engineering and is being applied in diverse fields such as agriculture, medicines environment, etc.

Over the past two decades, biotechnology has developed rapidly and world economy has become more globalised and liberalized (Hosseini et al., 2012). In agriculture field, biotechnology is being used to invent new plant varieties with the qualities of high yield, resistance to pest, resistance to viruses and capacity to withstand drought conditions. A new and improved variety of plant possessing different characteristics features can be produced though manipulation of genes or incorporation of foreign genes into the cells of existing plants. This process is called as genetic engineering. e.g. the varieties of plants such as *BT* cotton, *BT* rice, *BT* soyabean are produced through genetic engineering.

Biotechnology is being applied on animals in different ways. Inside an animal body many proteins are produced that are useful in the manufacture of drugs and medicines. Through biotechnology proteins produced inside the body of the animal can be identified and can be produced industrially to use in the manufacture of drugs and medicine .moreover biotechnologically produced animals can be used in testing new medicine and curing processes e.g. Oncomouse, the animals invented through biotechnology is used for cancer testing. Animals are used as bioreactors to produced human metabolic products. e.g. Tracy a sheep whose germline contains a genetic construction comprising a human gene plus 'promoter'. As a result Tracy's milk gland produces proteins identical to human ones. Examples of such protein are human insulin, relaxin hormones.

Biotechnology is being used to produce new drugs, medicines surgical processes and diagnostic methods. In 1982, genetically engineered insulin approved for use in diabetics in U.K. and U.S.A. in nineteen eighties, genetically engineered growth hormone, approved for treatment of dwarfism, new antibiotics have been produced by genetically engineered organism, genetically engineered proteins used to treat heart attacks and strokes, new vaccines are invented foot and mouth disease, monoclonal antibodies employed to boost the body's defense against cancer and other diseases were introduced. The process of gene therapy was used in the treatment of hereditary. Biotechnology represents a powerful alternative pharmaceuticals method of drug which as practised for the most this century involved the laborious screening of thousands of organic compounds found naturally in soil, plants and moulds. For cleaning up of pollutants in the environment, microorganisms produced through biotechnology can also be used. This has come to limelight when Dr. Anant Chakraborty, a Microbiologist in America invented a microorganism capable of splitting the oil pollutants in the environment (Dennis, 1981).

The public-private partnerships are highly desirable in developing countries, in order to harness the benefit of biotechnology. Public sector has a role in basic and strategic research and it can collaborate with private sector in assessing social and economic conditions. It could also facilitate the process of acquiring legal permission and providing infrastructural resources (Hosseini et al., 2012). The goal of partnerships is not to transform public sector institutions into private companies. The private sector is unlikely to replace the role of public sector in research or in facilitating broad application of biotechnology in developing countries (Lewis, 1999). Rather the role of the public sector will remain vital, as the private sector is unlikely to deliver biotechnology applications for many crops grown by the poor farmers and orphan crops and to address all biotic and abiotic production constraints important in developing countries. It is the responsibility of public sector to fill these gaps. Moreover, the public sector will continue to provide a critical role in addressing broad policy issues, and guiding programs that optimize public benefits from technological innovations in agriculture (Khush, 2007).

Evolution of Patent Law in concern with Biotechnology

The evolution of patent law dates back nineteen sixties. In famous "Red Dove" case of 1969, which confirmed rejection by the German Patent Office of a method for breeding Doves with red plumage only on the grounds that method was not repeatable. In fact it was the first case to open the doors to patenting of biotechnological inventions, as these eligible for patent protection if they met the criteria for patentability. In the early seventies in Europe, issues relating to biotechnology inventions have raised eyebrows. In the early 1970s German Federal Supreme Court upheld patent protection for new microorganisms, if the inventor were to demonstrate a reproducible for its generation.

However, the path breaking decision of patenting of biotechnology inventions can be found in Chakraborty's case. In 1972, Ananda M. Chakraborty, a microbiologist, filed for a patent application assigned to the General Electric Company. This application asserted thirty-six claims related to Chakraborty's invention, genetically engineered bacteria capable of breaking down multiple components of crude oil. Such properties are not possessed by any naturally existing bacteria. The patent examiner allowed the first two claims involving the process and the carrier material, but rejected the third claim for patentability of the bacteria on the ground that there was no coverage for the bacteria within section 101 of the patent law. The examiner reasoned that the claimed microorganisms were "products of nature" and thus not patentable because living things, generally, were not patentable subject matter. The Patent Office Board of Appeals also rejected the claim. Finally the issue reached the Supreme Court. Chief Justice Burger delivering the opinion of the court held that; Chakraborty's microorganism is not available naturally, it is human made and it is novel invention capable of industrial application, hence is eligible for patent. After this decision USPTO started issuing patents on biotechnology inventions. It has affected the Patent canopy to be extended to cover biotechnology inventions 9 (Dennis, 1981).

Table 1. Examples of life science inventions which may be eligible for patenting

Area		Patentable inventions
Genetic Engineering	·	Isolated DNA sequences and proteins to which functions have been ascribed
	·	Unique sequences of the nucleotides or amino acids that have been uncovered
	·	Vectors containing nucleotide sequences and cells containing the vectors
Microbiological Science	·	Genetically Modified Organisms used in the processes such as fermentation or brewing
	·	New microbes that have been isolated, purified and cultured, provided they must fulfill the patent requirements
Plant and Animal Science	·	Genetically modified animals and plants
Diagnostics	·	Primers used for diagnostic purpose
	·	Diagnosis Kits containing such primers
	·	SNPs and ESTs used for diagnostics
	·	Novel antigens and receptors that are newly located
	·	Novel monoclonal antibodies and immunological tests
Pharmaceuticals	·	Novel purified chemicals or pharmaceuticals
	·	Pharmaceutically accepted isomers and salts of compounds
	·	Novel pharmaceutical carriers
	·	Crude extracts of pharmaceutically important natural compounds
Medical Science	·	Instruments for use in surgeries, diagnostics or therapy

Patenting of plants and related inventions

The journey of patent law in patenting of biotechnology inventions has not confined just to microorganisms, but it has continued to extend to patent protection of transgenic plants and related inventions. In 1986, in Expart Hibberd, the U.S. patent office board of appeals overtuned the refusal of a patent examiner had argued that the invention was product of nature. With this decision the USPTO began issuing patents protecting biotechnological inventions in plants. After this decision, *BT* Cotton and *BT* rice were patented in 1992 and *BT* soyabean in1994. Since the development of the first transgenic plants, a wide diversity of patents have been sought on all aspects of the process, ranging from the underlying tissue culture methods by introducing the heterologous DNA, and to the composition of the DNA construct so introduced (Kesan, 2000).

The plant science inventions that may be eligible for patent protections can be briefly enumerated. Though essential biological processes for the production of plants cannot be patented, new plant varieties produced by conventional breeding, may be protected through Plant Breeder's Rights. Similarly, genetically modified plant varieties are also considered patentable in UK, Europe and USA. Commercial production of any GM crop variety requires many of patents and licenses. It is only the big companies that can afford to put together the IPR portfolios necessary to give them the freedom to operate (Barton, 1997). In addition, now, under the Trade-Related Aspects of Intellectual Property Rights (TRIPS) agreement of the World Trade Organization, most developing countries are required to put in place their own IPR systems, including IPR for plants (Giannakas, 2001).

Patenting of Animals

Patenting of animal models is the need of hour, because it is an indispensable tool for screening of novel molecule to various diseases. A human pathological condition in animals is most important to determine the therapeutic efficacy of novel molecule. They allow facilitation of the screening process to eliminate inactive moieties and assess the pharmacologist to identify the therapeutic potential and characterize the toxicological profile of novel chemical or biological entities (Kandhare et al., 2011). The standards for patentability of animal biotechnological inventions must be determined responsibly and evaluated accurately (Koopman, 2002). In 1987 USPTO issued a statement where it stated: The USPTO now considers non-naturally occurring, non human, multicellular living organisms, including animals to be patentable subject matter within the scope of 35 U.S.C. 101 (Dennis, 1981).

On the basis of this policy; USPTO granted first patent on an animal, the Harvard Oncomouse in 1988. In the Harvard Oncomouse case, the claim was a genetically modified mouse useful for cancer testing. The patent was granted, as the Oncomouse was non-naturally occurring, non human, multicellular being. With this decision, animal inventions have become patentable subject matter. After this case, the mice race continued tens of patents have been granted on inventions relating to transgenic mice. On the same line, transgenic sheep producing targeted protein milk, pigs producing low cholesterol meat and animals that produce pharmaceuticals in bioreactors were patented. The Indian Patent Law section 3i and 3j states that all the surgical processes and animals are not patentable, hence animal models are not patentable in India. If the suitable amendments are made then animal models can be patentable in India and it would open novel vistas in the research arena in India (Bagle et al., 2012).

Patenting of Cells and Genes

The advent of recombinant DNA technology, gene splicing, gene manipulation have poised towards the patenting of cells and genes. Cell is considered as the microorganism, which is a part of every living being plant or animal or human being. Cell has the capacity of self replication and can grow into number of cells. Patenting human genes and stem cells is generally perceived as ethically controversial. Many of the gene patents submitted are too broad, granting the inventor rights over all future applications of a particular DNA sequence. Instead of stimulating research, such patents often straitjacket both research and diagnosis.

In 1984, 'Moore cell line', producing valuable antimicrobial and cancer fighting protein, was granted patent. Here onwards, the patenting human cells, genes and gene sequences were started. In US and Australia, apart from human beings and the biological processes for their generations, all other inventions relating to animal or animal part are patentable, subject to overall exceptions on morality and public order (Danish Council of Ethics. 2000). Indian Patent Act, 1970 was not allowing patenting of living things. However, having signed TRIPS Agreement, India has brought changes in its Patent Law. Under Indian Patent Act, patents are made available for biotechnological inventions (TRIPS, 1994).

Examples of life science inventions which may be eligible for patenting (http:// www.svw.co.za/patents-biotech.html) are enlisted in Table 1

Social considerations and concerns in patenting biotechnology

It is widely considered that commercialization of biotechnology, especially research and development, by transnational pharmaceutical and agri-biotech companies is already excessive and is increasingly dangerous to distributive justice, human rights and access of marginal populations to basic human goods (Cahill, 2001). Researchers in many developing countries are unaware of the proper patenting procedure. With the lack of understanding there is usually no proper IPR strategy, which includes proper documentation of all invention. The task of seeking protection of intellectual property rights (IPRs) created in the course of research and the commercialization of inventions can become costly, tedious, and at times, not even viable because of the time lag from the bench to the marketplace.

Agricultural point of view

Although transgenic animals have much to offer to the productivity and quality of farm animals, small family farmers fear allowing patents on transgenic animals will push them out of the market. The economically desirable increased productivity sounds like financial ruin to small family farms. Because genetically created animals will likely be expensive, small farmers fear that a small number of large cooperations will be able to corner the market, thereby depriving the small family farms of their livelihood.

Additionally, the farmers are concerned that the initial acquisition price of genetically altered animals, and the subsequent royalties, will increase rather than decrease the costs for farmers and consumers. This position is fairly weak, however, because the transgenic farm animals will be stronger and more disease resistance and should balance the cost of initial investment. Proponents of animal patents additionally point out that the patent protection for the transgenic animals may actually help the farmers. This argument suggests that without PTO issued protection, the owners of the transgenic animal will licence their animals selectively, resulting in a small concentration of significantly advantaged, commercialised farming (Nature, 2003).

Environmental point of view

Some environmental groups are concerned with the fact that we do not have clear ideas of what could happen if these transgenic animals were set free in the environment. The National Wildlife Foundation (NWF) opposes patenting for transgenic animals because of the lack of legislation in the area concerning their release into the wild life. Although rejecting patent application for transgenic animals does not mean the creation and release of such animals to be prohibited, the NWF fears that allowing patents will cause greater number of transgenic animals to be created, and thus increasing the risk to ht environment.

However, biotechnology is capable of so many public benefits that it should not be stifled by denying its patent application. The concern of the NWF and other environmentalists are valid; however which is why, EPA (Environment Protection Act) should review the appropriateness of biotechnology practice. If necessary, regulations regarding the creation and release of transgenic animals could be easily created. Requiring the PTO to decide the possible environmental consequences of furthering biotechnology research again takes the PTO out of its role of deciding novelty, utility and non- obviousness (Nature, 2003).

Animal rights point of view

Concerns about the cruel treatment of animals are quiet prevalent in discussion about transgenic animals. It is true that many of the animals engineered to help in human disease research are bred to suffer from such diseases like AIDS, sickle cell anaemia and cancer. Although it is unpleasant to consider the experimental condition that these transgenic animals must endure, denying patent protection will not ease their suffering. It is unquestionable that some animal suffer with transgenic research; however, animals may suffer even more with traditional animal research. Denying patents for transgenic animals will not stop the research. Those truly concerned with animal rights in transgenic research should ask to regulate the type of research performed, and not the patent protection extended (http://www.wipo.int/wipo_magazine/en/2006/03/article_0006.html).

Moral and Religious concerns

The opponents to patenting biotechnology based on moral and religious concerns seem to be much more opposing to the existence of science, rather than the existence of patents for the discoveries. The general concern is that research in biotechnology is "playing GOD" and undermining the "Sanctity of life" as GOD created it. This position looses site of the fact that the biotechnological research is performed to help the human condition rather than harm it. It is usually not the issuance of patents that evokes the moral dilemma, but rather misconceptions about biotechnology.

SUMMARY

Biotechnology is a blooming industry in many developing countries, including agriculture and health sciences, patents play a key role in R&D and product development. Scientific research can benefit from patents, apart from providing protection for inventions. Moreover, recognition and understanding of the importance of patents do not always coincide; many factors discourage use of patent information, including difficulty of access, amount of time involved, difficulty in reading documents and inability to fully understand the information. Because of increasing importance and emphasis on patents, in the non-profit sector as well as the for-profit sector, scientists are well-advised to become familiar with basics of intellectual property, especially patents. Merits and demerits of any technology go hand in hand, but one should take the positive aspect of IPRs to deliver fruitful impact on research and development.

REFERENCES

1. Bagle T.R., Kunkulol RR, Baig MS, More SY (2012). Transgenic animals and their application in medicine. Int J Med Res Health Sci. 2:107-116.

2. Barton, J. (1997). Appendix A: Intellectual property and regulatory requirements affecting the commercialization of transgenic plants. In Transgenic Plants (Galun, E. and Breiman, A., eds), pp. 254-277. London: Imperial College Press.

3. Cahill, L.S. (2001). Genetics, commodification, and social justice in the globalization era. Kennedy Inst. Ethics J. 11, 221-238.

4. Dennis J. Walsh Diamond v. Chakrabarty: Oil Eaters: Alive and Patentable, 8 Pepp. L. Rev. 3 (1981)

5. Diamond v. Chakrabarty, 447 U.S. 303 (1980).

6. Danish Council of Ethics. (2000). Consultative reply concerning a draft bill on an amendment to the Patents Act (L 66). Submitted on 11 May 2000. Appendix 10 of the Council's Danish annual report from 2000.

7. Graff G., Heiman A., and Zilberman, D. (2002). University research and offices of technology transfer Californian Mgt Rev 45, 88-115.

8. Giannakas, K. (2001). The Economics of Intellectual Property Rights Under Imperfect Enforcement: Developing Countries, Biotechnology, and The Trips Agreement. EPTD Discussion Paper No. 80.Washington: International Food Policy Research Institute.

9. Hosseini S.J.F., Nejad S.B., and Najafabadi M.O. (2012), Role of public sector in developing agricultural biotechnology in Iran. Afr J Biotechnol 11, 13560-13563.

10. Huskisson, F.M. (1996), Patents and biotechnology. In Transgenic Plants:A Production System for Industrial and Pharmaceutical Proteins (Owen, M.R.L. and Pen, J., eds), pp. 313-328. New York: Wiley.

11. Kandhare AD, Raygude KS, Ghosh P, Gosavi TP, Bodhankar SL. (2011). Patentability of Animal Models: India and the Globe. International Journal of Pharmaceutical and Biological Archives.; 2:1024-32.

12. Khush G., (2007). Biotechnology: Public-Private Partnership and IPR in the context of developing countries. In: Biodiversity and the Law: Intellectual Property, Biotechnology and Traditional Knowledge (McMains C. eds.) pp. 179-191, London U.K. Earthscan.

13. Kesan J. P. (2000). Intellectual property protection and agricultural biotechnology, a multidisciplinary perspective. Am. Behav. Sci. 44, 464-503.

14. Koopman J., (2002). The Patentability of Transgenic Animals in the United States of America and the European Union: A Proposal for Harmonization. In: Fordham Intellectual Property, Media and Entertainment Law Journal New York U.S.A

15. Kumar A and Das G. (2010). Biodiversity, Biotechnology and Traditional Knowledge: Understanding Intellectual Property Rights, Narosa, New Delhi.

16. Lesser W. (1997). The Role of Intellectual Property Rights in Biotechnology Transfer under the Convention on Biological Diversity ISAAA Briefs No. 3. ISAAA: Ithaca, NY. pp. 22.

17. Lewis J. (1999). "Leveraging partnership between the public and private sector experience of USAID's agricultural biotechnology program". Agricultural biotechnology for the poor. Proceedings from an international conference. CGIAR. October 21-22.

18. Nature, (2003). Gene patents and the public good p. 207.

Chapter-4

PROTECTION OF IDEAS BY INTELLECTUAL PROPERTY RIGHTS IN THE FIELD OF BIOTECHNOLOGY

PRAGYA SAXENA AND D. S. RATHORE

Department of Biotechnology, Govt. K.R.G. P.G. College, Gwalior

Intellectual property (IP) rights are the rights given to persons over the creations of their minds. They usually give the creator an exclusive right over the use of his/her creation for a certain period of time. Protected IP rights like other property can be a matter of trade, which can be owned, sold or bought. These are intangible and non-exhausted consumption.

As in other fields of technology, there is a need for legal protection in respect of biotechnological inventions also. Such inventions are creations of the human mind just as much as other inventions, and are generally the result of substantial research, inventive effort and investment in sophisticated laboratories. Typically, enterprises engaged in research only make investments if legal protection is available for the results of their research. As with other inventions, there is an obvious need for the protection of biotechnological inventions, not only in the interest of inventors and their employers, but also in the public interest in order to promote technological progress. Legal protection of inventions is normally effected through the grant of patents or other titles. However, inventors in the field of biotechnology are faced with several obstacles when seeking protection for their inventions. These obstacles do not exist to the same degree in other areas of technology. This review paper mainly focuses on the tools/types of IP rights and pooling of patents that can be used in protection of idea for Biotechnological inventions.

INTRODUCTION

Imagination is more important than knowledge - Albert Einstein

Intellectual property is of considerable, and growing, importance to global economies. IP remains an interesting, fast developing, and vast subject in the practice of law. Intellectual property remains a God given asset that results from man's innovation, ingenuity and zeal to stretch his intellect in the quest for knowledge and a better future. Intellectual Property right, is the term used to describe the branch of law which protects the application of thoughts, ideas and information which are of commercial value. It thus covers the law relating to patents, copyrights, trademarks, trade secrets and other similar rights **(Cornish, 1989).**

Intellectual property, very broadly, means the legal rights which result from intellectual activity in the industrial, scientific, literary and artistic fields. Countries have laws to protect intellectual property for two main reasons. One is to give statutory expression to the moral and economic rights of creators in their creations and the rights of the public in access to those creations. The second is to promote, as a deliberate act of Government policy, creativity and the dissemination and application of its results and to encourage fair trading which would contribute to economic and social development (**WIPO intellectual property handbook, 2008).**

Intellectual property is traditionally divided into two branches, "industrial property" and "copyright." The Convention Establishing the World Intellectual Property Organization (WIPO), concluded in Stockholm on July 14, 1967 (Article 2(viii)) provides that "intellectual property shall include rights relating to:

- literary, artistic and scientific works,
- performances of performing artists, phonograms and broadcasts,
- inventions in all fields of human endeavour,
- scientific discoveries,
- industrial designs,
- trademarks, service marks and commercial names and designations,
- protection against unfair competition,

and all other rights resulting from intellectual activity in the industrial, scientific, literary or artistic fields."Intellectual property as a concept of protection of idea falls within the functional approach definition of Professor **David Allan** when he said: *"Anything that performs the function of security must be a security"* .In recent years, society has witnessed an explosive growth in biotechnology research. This growth has been attributed to many factors, among others, the completion of the human genome project, the success of animal cloning, pharmaceutical research, and other notable advances **(Sampson M., 2002).** These recent advances promise to further our standard of living by benefiting medicine, agriculture and industry. As a result of the scramble to gain proprietary rights over these advances, the biotechnology field has seen phenomenal growth in the number of biotechnology patents that have been filed **(Hasson A.I., 2002).**

The development of the genetic resources of biodiversity is known as biotechnology. Broadly defined, biotechnology includes any technique that uses living organisms or parts of organisms to make or modify products, to improve plants or animals, or to develop microorganisms for specific uses **(Uebler, E. A. 1990)**. Mankind has used forms of biotechnology since the dawn of civilization. However, it has been the recent development of new biological techniques (e.g., recombinant DNA, cell fusion, and monoclonal antibody technology) which has raised fundamental social and moral questions and created problems in intellectual property rights. Intellectual property protection for biotechnology is currently in a state of flux. Whilst it used to be the case that living organisms were largely excluded from protection, attitudes are now changing and increasingly biotechnology is receiving some form of protection. These changes have largely taken place in the USA and other industrialized countries, but as other countries wish to compete in the new biotechnological markets, they are likely to change their national laws in order to protect and encourage investment in biotechnology **(Groombridge B., ed. 1992)**.

According to the **Report of the Secretary's Advisory Committee on Genetics, Health and Society, 2010,** assessing a biotechnology invention is more challenging because of three main reasons. First, biotechnology is a field of applied biology and involves biology and chemistry, however, in many instances it also dependents on the knowledge and method from outside the sphere of biology. Second, claims of biotechnology inventions are very complex in nature and which forces a judge or patent examiner to deal with very fundamental issues such as the significance of the term "human" in describing a protein. And third, it raises important policy questions **(HUGO Intellectual Property Committee, 2000)**. In the techno-legal research, technical analysis of biotechnology information related to patents is carried out with the help of various biotechnology information resources and patent-informatics tools **(McGough *et al*, 1992)**.

Forms and Operation of Traditional IPR Systems: (Lesser, 1997)

IPR systems traditionally include five forms of legislation: patents, Plant Breeders' Rights, copyright, trademarks, and trade secrets. Of those, patents, PBRs, trademark and trade-secrets, both singly and combined, are directly applicable to applications under the Convention and receive attention here.

Patents: Patents, like other forms of IPR, operate as a balance between the inventor and society. Society grants a temporary, partial monopoly to the inventor. Temporary refers to the duration of protection, generally about 20 years; and partial describes the scope of protection, the degree of difference required before a related development is not covered by the patent.

Plant Breeders' Rights: Plant Breeders' Rights is a specialized patent-like system for cultivated plants. PBRs were first systematized in 1961 under the International Union for the Protection of New Varieties of Plants (UPOV). In place of the novelty, non-obviousness, and utility requirements of patent law, PBRs use distinctness, uniformity, and stability (DUS). Uniformity and stability are measures of reproducibility true-to-form, respectively among specimens within a planting as well as between generations. The principal test then is distinctness, that the variety be "clearly distinguishable" from all "known varieties". PBRs are further distinguishable from patents by the allowance of so-called "farmers' privilege" and "research exemption," sometimes called "breeders' privilege." The farmers' privilege is the right to hold materials as a seed source for subsequent seasons (farmer saved-seed or bin competition), something which would generally be an infringement with patented materials. The research exemption refers to the right to use protected materials as the basis for developing a new variety or other research use. Research or experimentation under patents is not as well defined but is generally believed to be fairly broad. Because of these differences, PBRs are generally considered to provide less protection than patents.

Trade Secrets: Trade secrets, to describe them in their simplest terms, assist in the maintenance of secrets by imposing penalties (the recovering of costs) when information held as secret is improperly acquired or used. Unlike patents and the like, no formal application procedure is needed for a trade secret; rather the information must have some commercial value, and an effort be made to keep it secret. As long as these conditions are met, protection can be permanent.

Trademarks: Trademarks are the reservation of a word, symbol, or phrase in association with a product or service. In effect the trademark name represents the product to consumers, justifying an investment in its identification. From a theoretical and economic perspective, trademarks assist customers in identifying products of consistent, often high quality. Trademarks are permanent as long as they remain in use, are identified as such, and do not acquire a generic connotation. Often a trademark, such as Coca-Cola, is the most valuable asset of a corporation. Within agriculture, trademarks can be associated with products at the firm level (Pioneer Hi-Bred), or individual products such as the FlavrSavr™ tomato. Note that the tomato variety, McGregor®, is also protected, so the two forms of IPR are, in that instance, complementary **(Lesser, 1997).**

One of the biggest public concerns voiced against the granting of patents by the United States Patent Office (USPTO) to inventions in biotechnology, specifically inventions based on genetic information, is the potential lack of reasonable access to that technology for the research and development of commercial products and for further basic biological research. One possible solution lies in the formation of patent pools **(Clark, 2000).**

Patent pool

A "patent pool" is an agreement between two or more patent owners to license one or more of their patents to one another or third parties. **(Klein, 1997)** Alternatively, a patent pool may also be defined as "the aggregation of intellectual property rights which are the subject of cross-licensing, whether they are transferred directly by patentee to licensee or through some medium, such as a joint venture, set up specifically to administer the patent pool."Over the last one hundred and fifty years, patent pools have played an important role in shaping both the industry and the law in the United States **(Carlson, 1999).**

Legal Guidelines for forming Intellectual Property Pools

Since 1977, the Antitrust Division of the U.S. Department of Justice has had an official regulatory procedure for reviewing various types of business practices proposed by private firms. **(Brunetti, 1997)** Since 1979, the FTC has had a similar procedure, in which businesses may seek FTC advisory opinions concerning proposed business practices. These procedures led to Justice Department and FTC policies in the intellectual property licensing area, and in 1995, these agencies issued *Antitrust Guidelines for the Licensing of Intellectual Property ("IP Guidelines"),* which sets forth their enforcement policies in this area. The IP Guidelines specifically address pooling arrangements involving intellectual property owners and their rights. In particular, the IP Guidelines state that intellectual property pooling is precompetitive when it:

(1) Integrates complementary technologies,

(2) Reduces transaction costs,

(3) Clears blocking positions,

(4) Avoids costly infringement litigation, and

(5) Promotes the dissemination of technology **(U.S. Dep't of Justice & Fed. trade Comm'n, 1995).**

The IP Guidelines also discuss that excluding firms from an intellectual property pool may be anticompetitive if:

(1) The excluded firms cannot effectively compete in the relevant market for the good incorporating the licensed technologies,

(2) The pool participants collectively possess market power in the relevant market, and

(3) The limitations on participation are not reasonably related to the efficient development and exploitation of the pooled technologies.

Anticompetitive effects may also occur if the pooling arrangement deters or discourages participants from engaging in research and development which is more likely "when the arrangement includes a large fraction of the potential research and development in an innovation market."

The Justice Department has applied these guidelines in considering and approving three proposed patent pools. Its first review set forth the following additional guidelines:

(1) The patents in the pool must be valid and not expired,

(2) No aggregation of competitive technologies and setting a single price for them,

(3) An independent expert should be used to determine whether a patent is essential to complement technologies in the pool,

(4) The pool agreement must not disadvantage competitors in downstream product markets, and

(5) The pool participants must not collude on prices outside the scope of the pool, e.g., on downstream products. Currently, the guidelines have been "collapsed" into the following two overarching questions:

(i) "whether the proposed licensing program is likely to integrate complementary patent rights," and

(ii) "if so, whether the resulting competitive benefits are likely to be outweighed by competitive harm posed by other aspects of the programmes" **(Clark et al., 2000).**

Benefits from the Pooling of Biotechnology Patents

The first benefit, associated with the pooling of patents, is the elimination of problems caused by "blocking" patents or "stacking" licenses **(Heller et al., 1998).** In biotechnology, the granting of patents to nucleic acids may create blocking patents or lead to stacking licenses. By creating a patent pool of basic patents, businesses can easily obtain all the necessary licenses required to practice that particular technology concurrently from a single entity. This, in turn, can facilitate rapid development of new technology since it opens the playing field to all members and licensees of the patent pool **(Clark et al., 2000).** Patent pools can eliminate the problems associated with blocking patents or stacking licenses in the field of biotechnology, while at the same time encouraging the cooperative efforts needed to realize the true economic and social benefits of genomic inventions **(Sung et al., 1998).** The second benefit, is that patent pools have the potential to significantly reduce several aspects of licensing transaction costs **(Merges, 1999).** For example, patent pools can reduce or eliminate the need for litigation over patent rights because such disputes can be easily settled, or avoided, through the creation of a patent pool. A reduction in patent litigation would save businesses time and money, and also avoid the uncertainty of patent rights caused by litigation **(Carlson, 1999).**

Biotechnology Patents- an Access to Knowledge and ethical issues:

The biotechnology patents cover three types of matter, *viz.,*

- Products of biotechnology (e.g., seeds, drugs, diagnostic kits);

- Methods and processes of making the biological matter (e.g., fermentation, gene splicing, methods of controlling pests);

- Uses of biological matter (living or non-living) (e.g., antibodies, enzymes, DNA molecules).

The basic problem in granting patents was that much of the biotechnology knowledge was not directed to products of end use. Other objections to patenting genes were:

- They are discoveries (identifying something that already exists) and not inventions;

- Products of nature are not new;

- The basic core of humanity should not be owned by anyone as property.

However, two 1980 decisions of the U.S. Supreme Court changed all that. The Diamond vs. Chakraborty case was about patentability of a genetically modified bacterium. The court held that such material is patentable because there is novelty. Subsequent, gene or DNA patents have claims that they cover nucleotide sequences that encode genes or fragments of genes. For example, Human Genome Sciences in the U.S. claimed a patent for a gene though its function was not known. It was only asserted that it will be a research reagent or material for diagnostics. Subsequently it was discovered that it was the docking receptor CCR5 used by the HIV virus to infect a cell. Similarly, the U.S. Supreme Court ruled that genetically altered life forms require patenting. A decision by the court allowing an oil company to patent an oil eating microorganism set a precedence and opened up massive possibilities, including that of the exploitation of genetic engineering for commercial purposes. **Lakshmikumaran and Pillai (2005)** pointed out that the Calcutta high court decision in the Dimminaco A.G. vs. Controller of Patents and designs had a similar basis (**Rao, 2007**).

Ethical issues: There are two basic approaches to applying patent law to biotechnology inventions. One is that the normal patentability criteria shall apply to everything, that is, the invention has the attributes of novelty, non-obviousness, utility and the invention should be deposited in a recognised depository. The second is to have a specific exclusion on certain types of invention **(Macer, 2000)**.

Some ethical issues in patenting in scientific research include

- Is the principle of beneficence, or loving good, served more by having research than by not having research?

- Do we encourage more research into more beneficial areas of science by the incentive system of patents than we would by not having patents?

- Is justice served by systems of intellectual property protection?

- What are the tolerable limits of doing harm by research subject, e.g. animals including humans?

- What are the tolerable limits of doing harm by rigid enforcement of patents if price becomes a barrier to use of a product by persons in need?

- Ethically can anyone own a product of their mind, a product of nature, a product of a designed process, a discovery or even an invention?

- Does it make any difference whether the product or process involves living organisms or rocks?

- Should we expect the practical law to share the same goals as that of ethics, namely can we expect ideal ethical laws or some compromise?

Relevant to this discussion of what is morality, is the weight of public opinion. There is public rejection of the idea of patenting animals in many countries, as seen in the International Bioethics Survey I conducted in 1993 in ten countries in Asia-Pacific **(Macer, 1994)**.

CONCLUSION

Your fortunes will come from your ideas - Robert Kiyosaki

Four forms of "traditional" IPR legislation are applicable for protecting the kinds of technologies, including biotechnology. These four, which can be used separately or jointly, include patents, Plant Breeders' Rights, trademarks, and trade secrets. Each is intended for a particular function and as such has specific attributes and exacting granting requirements. Certainly it is not possible to protect every form of innovation. As noted, IPRs are intended principally to foster private R&D. The available evidence generally supports that expectation; IPRs do indeed encourage investment by the private sector, especially for easily copied inventions. IPR systems have costs, royalty payments being the most obvious, but the costs of the absence of protection in terms of denied or delayed access must be determined on a case-by-case basis.

REFERENCES

1. Allan David, (1989). *'Security: Some Mysteries, Myths, and Monstrosities'* 15 Monash U.L Review, page 345.

2. Brunetti A.C., (1997). *Wading Into Patent Pooling: The Clinton Justice Department is Becoming More Tolerant of High-Tech Patent-Sharing Deals*, Intellectual Property<http://www.ipmag.com/brunetti.html>.

3. Carlson S.C., (1999).Note, *Patent Pools and the Antitrust Dilemma,* 16 YALE J. ON REG. 359-373.

4. Clark J., Piccolo J., Stanton B., Tyson K., *Critharis M., Kunin S., (2000). Patent pools: a solution to the problem of access in biotechnology patents?* United States Patent and Trademark Office.

5. CORNISH W.R., (1989). *Intellectual Property: Patents, Copyright, Trade Marks and Allied Rights. 2nd edition. London, Sweet and Maxwell.*

6. Dykman H.T., (1964). *Patent Licensing within The Manufacturer's Aircraft Association* (MAA), 46 J. PAT. OFF. SOC'Y 646-648.

7. Groombridge B. ed., (1992). I*ntellectual property rights for biotechnology. In Global biodiversity: Status of the Earth's living resources,* 495-99. London: Chapman and Hall.

8. Hasson A.I.,(2002). *Patenting Biotechnology: Inherent Limits, Intell. Prop. & Tech.* F. 041901.

9. Heller M.A. & Eisenberg R.S.,(1998). Can Patents Deter Innovation? The *Anticommons in Biomedical Research,* 280 Science 698 .

10. HUGO (2000).Intellectual property committee statement on patenting of DNA sequences< http://www.hugo-international.org/img/ip_dna_2000.pdf>.

11. Klein J. I., (1997). An address to the American intellectual property law association, on the subject of *CROSS-LICENSING AND ANTITRUST LAW* , reprinted at http://www.usdoj.gov/atr/public/speeches/1123.html, 333 U.S. 287-313.

12. *Lakshmikumaran M. & P.Phillip, (2005).* "Patenting Biotechnology Innovations". Asian Biotechnology and Development Review, 7 (2): 25-41.

13. Lesser W., (1997). *"The Role of Intellectual Property Rights in Biotechnology Transfer under the Convention on Biological Diversity"*, Edited by: Anatole F. Krattiger, ISAAA, Briefs No. 3. ISAAA: Ithaca, NY.pp. 22.

14. Macer D. R. J.,(2000). *"Ethical issues in patenting scientific research"*, In *Proceedings of the International Conference of the Council of Europe on Ethical Issues Arising From the Application of Biotechnology.* Volume II. (Council of Europe), pp. 173-181.

15. Macer D.R.J., (1994). *"Bioethics for the People by the People"* (Christchurch: Eubios Ethics Institute.

16. McGough K.J. and Burke D.P.,(1992). *"A Case for Expansive Patent Protection of Biotechnology invention"*; Harvard Journal of Law & Technology; Volume 6.

17. Merges R.P., (1999). *"Institutions For Intellectual Property Transactions: The Case for Patent Pools"* <www.law.berkeley.edu/institutes/bclt/pubs/merges>.

18. Rao,(2007). *"Biotechnology Inventions and the Patent Regime"*, Asian Biotechnology and Development ,Review Vol. 9 No. 2, pp 109-121.

19. Report of the Secretary's Advisory Committee on Genetics,(2010). Health and Society; "Gene Patents and Licensing Practices and Their Impact on Patient Access to GeneticTests", http://oba.od.nih.gov/oba/SACGHS/reports/SACGHS_patents_report_2010.pdf.

20. Sung L.M. and Pelto D.J., (1998). *"Greater Predictability May Result in Patent Pools"* As the Federal Circuit Refines Scope of Biotech Claims, Use of Collective Rights Becomes Likely, NLJ , reprinted at http://www.ljx.com/patents/0622pools.html.

21. U.S. Dep't of Justice & Fed. trade Comm'n,(1995). *Antitrust Guidelines for the Licensing of Intellectual Property ("IP Guidelines"),* reprinted at http://www.usdoj.gov/atr/public/guidelines/ipguide.html.

22. Wetherell J.R. Jr., (2001). *"U.S. Biotechnology Patent Concepts"*, at http://cbdn.ca/patent.html.

23. Sampson M., (2000). *"The Evolution of the Enablement and Written Description Requirements under 35 U.S.C. §112 in the area of Biotechnology"*, 15 Berkeley Tech. L. J. 1233-1234.

24. WIPO INTELLECTUAL PROPERTY HANDBOOK, (2008). Second Edition, WIPO publication no. 489 (E) ISBN 978-92-805-1291-5 WIPO 2004.

25. Uebler E. A., (1990). *"New developments in biotechnology: Patenting life".* Compiled by the Office of Technology Assessment, Congress of the United States, Marcel Dekker, New York, pp.208.

Chapter-5

PLANT VARIETY PROTECTION THROUGH INTELLECTUAL PROPERTY RIGHT

SUDHIR KUMAR PATHAK & RAJENDRA SINGH RATHORE

Department of Botany, Govt. M., J. S. P. G. College, Bhind (M.P.)

Although many of the legal principles governing Intellectual property rights have evolved over centuaries, It was not until the 19th Centuaries that the term Intellectual property began to be used and not until the late 20th Century that it became common place in the majority of the world. Intellectual Property Rights on biological materials embodied in the Trade Related Intellectual Property Right. These rights provides a choice for protecting plant varieties. Members may choose from patents a sui-generis system or a combination of two. Article 27.3(b) of TRIPS insists that members are required to provide for protection of plant varieties either by patents are an effective sui-generis system. A draft on plant breeders and farmer's right bill was first developed at the M.S. Swaminathan Research Foundation at a National Diologue on Farmer's Right and Plant Genetic Resources held in 1994. This legislation was presented in he bill on 9th August 2001. The protection of Plant Varieties and Farmer's Right Act. 2001 has 11 chapters and 97 section plant variety protections confer an exclusive right to plant breeder to market a variety that he has developed.

Modern usage of the term intellectual property goes back at least as far as 1867 with the founding of the North German confederation whose constitution granted legislative power over the protection of intellectual property to be confederation. The organization subsequently relocated to Geneva in 1960, and was succeeded in 1967 with the establishment of the World Intellectual Property Organization (WIPO) by treaty as an agency of the United Nations. In India innovations and novel techniques were retained within the families and small social groups that developed them, and there was no other system of protecting their rights to the knowledge so generated. In 1856, the then Govt. of India introduced the Act of protection of inventions. Later patents and Designs Protection Act was passed in 1872. In 1883, the Protection of Invention Act was introduced.

Plant varieties and animal breeds are developed through years of painstaking and scientifically planned work. These entities therefore, should be regarded as intellectual properties of the breeders who have developed them. It may be argued that these entities are essentially derived from naturally occurring lines, but they usually represent a considerable reorganization of the existing gene combinations and skillfull selection work. Many countries recognize plant varieties as an intellectual property and grant a protection to them through a patent or a suitable form of plant breeders right (PBR) (section 21.7).

The stated objective of most intellectual property law is to promote progress. By exchanging limited exclusive rights for disclosure of inventions and creative works, society and the patentee copyrights owner mutually benefits and on incentive is created for inventors and authors to create and disclose their work. Some commentators have noted that the objective of intellectual property legislators and those who support its implementation appears to be absolute protection. IPR provides financial incentive, economic growth and morality.

Plant Breeder' s Rights (PBR)

The rights granted by the Government to a plant breeder, originator or owner of a variety to excude others from producing or commercializing the propagating material of that Variety for a minimum period of 15-20 years. A person holding PBR title to a variety can authorize other interested persons and organizations to produce and sell the propagating materiel of that variety. It is important that the object of protection in PBR is the variety ,and that genetic components and the breeding procedures are not protectable. In addition PBR systems also contain some form of breeders exemption and farmers privilege (sections 21.7.5 and 21.7.6).

The International Organization for Plant Variety Protection (ASSINSEL) was established in 1938 with the objective of persuading governments of different countries for introducing laws to protect plant varieties. The most significant event in the development of PBR systems was the effort to harmonize PBR laws of different countries through UPOV (Union International Pour la protection des abstentions Vegetales, International Union for Protection of New Plant Varieties.)

Requirements for PBR

Under the provisions of UPOV 1991 Act, a plant variety must satisfy the following four criteria for protection. Establishment of Commercial Novelty, Test of Distinctness, Test of Uniformity and stability.

A. **Establishment of Commercial Novelty:** The criterion of novelty requires that a variety should not have been commercially exploited for more than on year before the grant of PBR protection in India and 4 years outside India. For foreign varieties to be registered is India it is 6 years.

B. **Test of Distinctness:** it required that the new variety must be distinguishable from other varieties by one or more identifiable morphological, physiological or other characteristics.

C.   **Test of Uniformity:** in essential characteristics subject to variation expected from the particular features of its propagation.

D.   **Stability:** The essential characteristics remain unchanged after repeated cycles of propagation.

FARMERS PRIVILEGE:

PBR systems generally allow the farmers to use the material of a protected variety produced on their farm for planting of their new crop without any obligation to the PBR title holder. This exemption is usually referred to as farmers privilege. Under the UPOV 1978 Act, there was explicit provision for farmers privilege .It should be clearly understood that farmers privilege applies to the use of seed produced by a farmer for sowing his own fields. PBR however does not allow farmers to exchange seeds of protected varieties produced on their farms. Farmers privilege is a most important provision for countries like India. Where over 90% of the total cropped area is sown by seeds produced by the farmers themselves. A majority of the farmers are poor and will be subject to unjust economic burden if they are forced to pay a royalty on the seed produced and used by them.

FARMER' S RIGHTS

Agriculture began some ten thousands years ago. During this vast period of time genetic resources have been selected, developed, used and conserved by farmer families and farming communities of particularly the gene-rich developing countries. These same materials have been and are being collected, conserved and used as raw materials to evolve the modern high yielding varieties of various crops. It has been argued that the farmers should be allowed a share in this profit in recognition of their contribution by way of the development of germplasms of the various crops. This has been recognized by FAO (resolution no.5/89) as farmer's rights which arise from the past, present and future contributions of farmers in conserving, improving and making available plant genetic resources, particularly in the centres of origin and diversity .

The Necessities for PBR: The concept of PBR originated in the developed countries, where private companies have been important and major players in plant breeding and seed production and marketing. The main considerations for the development of PBR systems were as follows.

- It allows breeders to benefit from the varieties developed by them ,which in turn encourages plant breeding activities.

- Private sector is encouraged to invest in plant breeding and seed industry.

- Development of a new plant variety is as much of an innovation as invention of a machine and product.

In India is markedly different from that in west in that plant breeding activity is largely carried out by public sector institutions (Agriculture Universities and ICAR institutes and centres), and private sector is yet to emerge as a major player. It has been argued (Ghijsen 1998) by some Asian countries should evolve their own system of PBR -

- That recognizes community interests e.g. the informal seed system of open - pollinated varieties

- That extends in public interest the concept of essentially- derived variety to varieties developed from unprotected varieties developed by public institutions.

The Protection of plant varieties and farmer's Right Act 2001 (PPVFR, 2001)

India has now enacted its own PBR law called protection of plant varieties farmer's Right Act 2001. A draft on plant breeders and farmer's right bill was first developed at the M.S. Swaminathan Research Foundation at a National Dialogue on farmer's Right and Plant Genetic Resources held in 1994. This legislation was presented in the bill on 9th August 2001 by the Lok Sabha. The protection of plant varieties and Farmers Right Act, 2001 has 11 chapters and 97 section. The Act aims to provide for the establishment of an effective system for protection of plant varieties. The Act recognizes the farmer not just as a cultivator but also a conserver of the Agricultural gene pool and a breeder who has bred several successful varieties.

The main features of this act are follows:-

1. Registration of farmers varieties, extent varieties and new varieties of such genera and species as notified in the official Gazette by the Central Government.

2. A new variety shall be registered if it meets the criteria of novelty, distinctiveness, Uniformity and stability.

3. Any variety that involves any technology including gene use restriction and terminator technologies which is injurious to life or health of human beings, animals or plants shall not be registered.

4. A variety has been essentially- derived from an initial variety can be registered as a new variety.

5. The duration of protection of the varieties will be 15 year for the extent varieties, 18 year for varieties of trees and vines and 15 year for varieties of other crops.

6. Registration of a variety confers on the breeder of that variety or his successor or his agent or licensee an exclusive right to produce, sell, market, distribute, import or export the variety.

7. The provisions for researcher's rights allow any person to use any registered variety for research and for creation of new varieties, except essentially- derived varieties, without paying any royalty to the PBR holder.

8. Any farmer who is engaged in the conservation genetic resources of land races and wild relatives of economic plants and their improvement through selection and preservation shall be entitled of recognisition and reward from the Gene Fund. He shall be entitled to save, use, sow, resow, exchange, share or sell his farm produced including seed of a variety (section 39) protected under this Act, in the same manner as he was entitled before coming into force of this act.

9. The procedure for making a claim attributable to the contribution in the evolution of any variety and seeking reward from the gene fund has been specified.

10. The Central Govt. is to constitute a National Gene fund from the earnings of benefit sharing of registered varieties, compensations deposited in the fund, and contributions from National and International Organizations.

11. Compulsory license may be granted after 3 years of registration of a variety.

12. The Central Govt. shall establish the protection of plant varieties and Farmers Rights Authority.

13. The registry shall maintain a national register of plant varieties containing names of all registered varieties, names and addresses of their breeders and other relevant details.

14. The breeder shall be required to deposit specified quantities of seed or propagules of the registered variety.

15. Citizens of Conventions Countries will have the same rights as citizens of India Under the Act.

16. Application for registration of a variety may be made in India with in 12 months from the date of application for registration of the same plant variety made in a convention country.

In this way both farmers and breeders rights are protected. The opportunity to breeders of obtaining profits from varieties developed by them will act as an incentive in promoting plant breeding research and encourages private companies to invest in plant breeding activities. So the protect plant breeders right to stimulate investment for research and development both in the public and private sector for the development of a new plant varieties and to promote growth of seed industry to facilitate availability of high quality seeds and planting material to farmers.

REFERENCES

1. Ganguli, P. (1998). Patenting innovations: New demands as in emerging contexts Current Sci. 75.

2. Ghijsen, H.(1998). PVP essential to crop improvement in Asia Pacific. Asian Seed and Planting Material 5:31-33.

3. Gupta, P.K. (1996). Transgenic plants. Some current issues current sci. 70.

4. http://en.wikipedia.org./w/index.php_Intellectual Property

5. Kayande, N.V. and Patil S.P. (2008). India's plant variety protection and farmers Right Act, 2001. Agrobios News letter Vol. VI, No.8, January.

6. Singh, B.D. (2004). Biotechnology, expanding Horizons. Kalyani Publishers. Ludhiana.

Chapter-6

INTELLECTUAL PROPERTY RIGHTS & THEIR IMPORTANCE IN RESEARCH BUSINESS AND INDUSTRY

KRISHNAPAL SINGH CHAUHAN

M. L. B. Arts and Commerce College, Gwalior, (M.P.)

"Intellectual property" is an intellectual creation of intellectual human mind for example goodwill, trademark, patent etc. In other word we can say that intellectual property is quite different from real property or formal property. We can acquire the formal property by money but intellectual property cannot be acquired by this type, it can be invented or discovered. Formal property is limited on the earth but there is no limit of intellectual property. The right of which is connected with intellectual property is called intellectual property right.

We know very well that man is an intellectual creation of the god. Man always try to create intellectual property to use their mind, some example of intellectual property are as under-

"Copyright, a manuscript of book or article, a recorded sound etc. but such article is salable or transferable, subject to the copyright of its author which is a property in fiction not in fact as read property is."[1]

"Similarly, patent right is a right in some new invention or article created by its author or owner. The invented article has a form, it is salable or transferable but subject to the patent holders right only thus, patent right also is a fictional property and not a real property."[2]

Similar is the position of design right, which exists in building having a new design or a creation of any other real property, This right also substitute in the real property, it is not an independent property but only a fictional property.

Thus it must be noted and kept in mind unconfused that intellectual property is basically a creation of intellect or relates to intellect, it is a right pervaded in some property of real nature ,as such it is only a fictional property and not a real property even though it as pervading some real property.

Main features of intellectually property:

1. Intellectual property is not a real property.

2. It is more valuable right than the real property.

3. It is unlimited.

4. Price of intellectual property cannot be determined it may be different.

5. The person who creates an intellectual piece of work own it like any other tangible property.

Law of intellectual Property right

The exclusive right of a person enjoy intellectual property is called intellectual property right. The intellectual Property right protects the invention of inventors. The Law of trademark protects the trademark used by the traders or businessman. In other word we can say that without I.P.R. we cannot protect or save the intellectual property. There are many intellectual property rights. Intellectual property law has been developed to protect the intellectual property as has already been explained intellectual property is the creation of the intellect of human brain. Literacy work, music composition, inventions, coining of trademarks, creation of designs etc. are the examples of intellectual property created by the intellect of human brain.

TRIPs agreement aims at balancing the interests of various stakeholders, Including innovators producers and consumers in a manner that enhance "Social and economic welfare." As article 7 of the TRIPs agreement provides as follows:

"The protection and enforcement of intellectual property rights should can tribute to the promotion of technology innovation and to the transfer and dissemination of technology, to the mutual advantage of products and user of technological knowledge and in manner conducive to a social and economic welfare and to a balance of rights and obligations." [3]

Importance of I.P.R. in Research Business and Industry

1. Importance of I.P.R. in Research: we cannot deny the importance of I.P.R. in research we can say I.P.R. has a great importance in research. We can realize it. In case there will be no intellectual property right -

No one will do research because he will think if I do research one can theft his work only I.P.R. can prevent it. On the other side a research is dipped upon another research so without research we can't do next research. For example when we write a book we need some related material for that book without related material we cannot write a book or it will be very hard to write a book without the availability of related material. The same situation is in the research, without availability of primary data it is very hard to do research. In doctrinal research we also use primary data which is already available, Intellectual property Law encourage the researchers, authors etc. to disclose their creation to the public without any fear of the infringement of their creations by others. Protection of intellectual property right of the inventors over their inventions by intellectual property law not only protects the economic interest of the researchers but also the economic interest of the nation to which these owners of intellectual properties belong. Intellectual property law encourages the inventors to invent new inventions.

Importance of I.P.R. in Business

Intellectual property has immense economic value when it is put into practice and has the capability of effecting the market also. Every business is depend upon its unique identity and I.P.R. Play important role to maintain unique identity of every business. We can take example of coca cola business it has a great reputation in business sector from a long period. No one can copy it's name and design because of I.P.R. if someone copy it's logo or name will be punished by I.P.R. Law. Without I.P.R. any business cannot grow up.

"Intellectual property law confers upon the creator of intellectual property an exclusive right with respect to his intellectual property for a specified period. This exclusive right of the creator over his intellectual property includes his right to assign his intellectual property, or without assigning his intellectual property itself, transfer any interest in his intellectual property in the favor of any other person in consideration of monitory gain."[4]

Importance of I.P.R. in industry

Intellectual property right has a great importance in industry also. Industrial revolution in the human history is one such example, machines invented by the intellectual of human brain caused the mass production of the goods in short period of time and created a situation where supply exceeded the demand for the goods. Such situation effected the industrial revolution took place. As a matter of fact economic development of any nation is directly related to its industrial development. Where as industrial development itself depends upon the inventions invented by the intellect human brain. Invention as intellect properties are protected by the intellectual property law.

Industrial design is a example of I.P.R. related to industry. "Industrial design means only the features of shape. Configuration, pattern, ornament or composition of lines or color applied to any article whether in two dimensional or three dimensional or in both forms, by any industrial process or means whether manual, mechanical or chemical separate or combined which in the finished article appeal to and are judged solely by the eye ; but does not include any trademark. In the case of industrial designs the property consists in the exclusive right to apply the design registered under the statute."[5]

CONCLUSION

Intellectual property right has become more important in the recent past due to an unprecedented development in the field of business and industry particularly in the field of research. In the age of satellites and internet, any development that takes place in one corner of the world gets communicated to the other corner in no time. This gives rise to enormous possibility of unauthorized working of invention or piracy of industrial design research also at the international level in such situation rights of a person with respect to his intellectual property Law. Because unauthorized working of inventions or privacy of industrial design affects adversely not only the individual interest of the owners of intellectual property but also affects the economy of a nation to which the owner's intellectual property belongs. So in conclusion we can say that I.P.R. has an unbeatable importance in research business and industry without I.P.R. we cannot imagine a safe research, business and industry.

REFERENCES

1. Nagrajan R.K. "Intellectual property Law" Faridabad (Haryana) Allahabad Law agency(2004)p.1.

2. Nagrajan R.K. "Intellectual property Law" Faridabad (Haryana) Allahabad Law agency(2004)p.1.

3. Article 7 of TRIPs agreement.

4. Paul Meenu "Intellectual property Laws" Allahabad Law agency (2004) p.7.

5. Bhandari M.K. "Intellectual property Right" Allahabad, Central Law Publication (2010) p.4.

Chapter-7

ROLE OF INTELLECTUAL PROPERTY RIGHTS IN HUMAN DEVELOPMENT

RAJENDRA SINGH RATHORE & SUDHIR KUMAR PATHAK

Department of Botany, Govt. M. J. S. P. G. College, Bhind (M.P.)

Monetary profit is the single most potent motivating force for relentless toil, ingenuity and inventiveness of human. Therefore, scientist and governments have attempted, since long to devise ways. Intellectual property is the area of law that deal with protecting the rights of those who create original work. It covers everything's from original play and novels to inventions and company identification mark. The purpose of intellectual property laws are to encourage technologies and safeguards, literary, artistic scientific works, performance of artists, phonograms and broadcast etc, innovation in all fields of human endeavor. This is achieved by the requirements of disclosure for patents. It encourages investment in research and development efforts and provides consumer with a larger range of useful product.

Scientist, research directors and policy maker face complex questions decisions when managing intellectual property rights for research, business and industries. There are main mechanisms for protecting I.P.R. e.g. P.V.R, patents, trademark, trade secrets, industrial design and copyright. PVR, these rights are granted by the state to plant breeders to exclude others from producing or commercializing material of a specific plant variety for a at least time of 15 to 20 years. Plants are in the form of a certificate granted by a government. It gives the innovator to exclude others from imitating, manufacturing and selling the invention for commercial use during the specified period. There are three various types of patents, utility, design and plant patents. Trademarks protect the names and identifying marks of products and companies. The purpose of trademark is to make it easy for consumer to distinguish competitor from each others. Trademarks are automatically assumed once a business begins using a certain mark to identify its company. If they are satisfied with the purchase for example KODAK for photography goods and Zodiac for ready-made clothes. Trade secret, when the individual/ organization owning an intellectual property does not disclose the property and keeps it as a closely guarded secret to promote his/its own commercial interests it is called trade secret. The best guarded trade secret of the modern times concern the formulation of COCA COLA copyright, they give owners exclusive rights to reproduce their work. Publicly display or perform their work and create derivative works. Copyrights broadly include literacy, musical, dramatics, choreographic, pictorial graphics and sculptural works etc. owners are given economic rights to financially benefit from their work and prohibit others from doing so without their permission. It is important to realize that copyrights do not protect ideas, only how they are expressed.

Intellectual property is a product of mind. It is similar to the property like a building or a van where is the property owner may use his property or he wishes and nobody else can use his property without his permission as per Indian laws. Monetary profit is the single most potent motivating force for relentless toil, ingenuity and inventiveness of humans. Therefore, societies and governments have attempted since long to devise ways and means to reward their inventors and thereby promote inventiveness. Intellectual property arises from an application of intellect and is usually in the farm of an India, a concept, a design, a process etc, which ultimately be translated into an useful product. The chief problem with intellectual property is that they can be copied and used by others. Issues of generation protection and exploitation of intellectual property are assuming increasing importance.

In India, innovations and novel technique were retained within small social groups, which developed them, the then government of India, introduced the act of protection of inventions. This act was based on the British patent law (1852) in Indian was introduced patent act 1911. The currently operative act, The Indian patents act, was passed in 1970 and amended in 1999. Property rights are not absolutely protected in any society because of the principle of justice and for the sake of "public interest", "social need" and "public utility" societies can confiscate intellectual property. This act provides financial inceptive, economic growth and morality which are essential for economically, scientifically and sociologically development of human activities. The scope and extent of protection of intellectual property rights are being increasing by harmonized around the world for providing business opportunities to prefect and enforce their right globally.

FUNCTION

Nations system provided that intellectual property shall include rights relating to the following:-

1. Artistic, broadcast, commercial names, industrial design, innovation, literary, performance of artists, phonograms, scientific discoveries, service mark and trademarks in all fields of human endeavor.

2. The intellectual property is protected by and governed by appropriate notional legislations. The national legislation specifically described the inventions, which are the subject matter of protection and those which are excluded from protections.

Objectives of IPR

The stated objective of most intellectual property law is to promote progress. There is three main objectives of IPR-

- **Financial incentive:** These exclusive rights allow of IPR to benefit from the property they have created, providing a financial incentive for the creation of the an investment in intellectual property.

- **Economic growth:** IPR are essential to maintaining economic growth and social development.

- **Morality:** Everyone has the right to the protection the moral and material interests resulting from any scientific, literary or artistic production of which he is the author.

Principles of intellectual property rights

Usually IPRs are protected by the following legal theory:

Patents: A patent is in the form of a certificate granted by a government. It is a personal properties which can be licensed by the person/organization. It gives the innovator the right to exclude others from imitating, manufacturing, using, or selling during specified period. The chief requirements for the award of a patent are as follows:

- **Novelty:** The invention must be new, and should not be already a public knowledge.

- **Inventiveness:** The invention should not be obvious to a person skilled in the art and should represent an innovation.

- **Industrial application and usefulness:** The invention must have an a future industrial application, which should be useful to the society.

- **Patentability:** The Indian patent act(1970) does not allow patents for pharmaceutical and agrochemical products, while they are patentable is USA, European union, Japan etc. Genetically modified micro-organism, plants and animal are patentable in USA, but they are not patentable in India. It may be emphasized that the issue of patentability of a given subject matter is straight forward only in some cases.

- **Disclosure:** The inventor is required to describe his invention in sufficient detail so that a person of normal skill is able to reproduce it. In case of genetically modified organisms the disclosure of an invention gives an opportunity to other innovators to improve upon the original invention so that it becomes more efficient.

Preparation of patents

- An inventor prepares an application for a patent.

- The application is filed with the patents office of the country.

- The application is scrutinized by a competent person of the patents office.

- Anyone desiring to challenge the application files his objections to the patents office.

- The objections to and the counter arguments for the application are heard by a competent authority.

- In case an application is not challenged, the patent is awarded to the applicant.

A.   **Copyright:** Copyright is an exclusive right and gives its creator or owner if the rights are sold. That anyone doesn't change or use the work without the permission of the copyrighted work to perform or display the work publicly. Copyright was created to provide protection to composers, writers, authors and artists to protect their original work against those who copy; those who take and use the form in which the original work was expressed by the author. The best example of literary, scientific and artistic works include productions such as books, pamphlets and other writings, dramatic-musical works and choreographic works etc, computer program is another mode of expression. A computer program is produced by one or human authors but, in its final mode of expression, it can be understood directly only by a computer and not by human readers(Gupta,1999). In India, the copyright act, 1975 as amended is in 1999 in force. Literary work under the copyright act has been amended in 1994, which includes computer programmes tables and compilations including computer databases. The term of copyright for published work is for the lifetime of the author plus 60 years. Copyright act is under the charge of ministry of human resources and development.

B.   **Trademark:** A trademark is an identification symbol which is used in the course of trade to enable the public to distinguish on trader's goods from the similar goods of other traders. Symbol help the consumer identify products includes designs slogan, smell and in biotechnology research *in-vitro* equipments bear trademark that are well known to worker in fields. Commercial names and designations constitute another category of elements of intellectual property.

Trademark rights are so important that multinational companies spend large amount of money to maintain their respective trademarks around the world. Every country has different trademark laws. However, there are agreements to ensure that a company's trademark is one country is protected in another country. India has a trade and merchandise but enacted in 1958 that has been amended in 1999.

C.   **Trade secrets:** A trade secret is any information that gives company a competitive edge over competitors and which the company maintains as secret and away from public knowledge. Trade secrets often include private property information. Trade secret rights are mainly kept and enforced through agreements between employers and employees. Usually at the time employment begins an employer makes an employee sign an agreement that grants the employers trade secret protection. Trade secrets are more common in industry where scholarly duplication is not required. Trade secret in the area of biotechnology may include gene transfer parameters, hybridization condition, corporate merchandising plans and customer lists.

D. **Designs:** Designs means the features of shape, configuration, pattern etc. applied to an article or an object is protected and not the article or object itself. He gives those ideas conceived by him a material from as a pictorial illustration as a specimen, prototype or model. In India, the design act,1911 a amended in 1999 is in force, in which the feature are protected as design. The act confers exclusive right to apply a design to any article in any class in which the design is registered. An industrial design can be a two or three dimensional pattern used to produced a product, industrial commodity of handicrafts

E. **Geographical indications:** The geographical indications for object of the trade related intellectual property rights. Agreement have been described as indications which could be used to recognize that a goods has originated in a particular territory locality, where the given quality, reputation or other characteristic of goods are essentially attributable to its geographical origin. A recent instance of violations of possible geographical indication is the case of BASMATI rice of Indian and Pakistan origin. In the TRIPs, there is an important provision that if someone uses a geographical indication as a trademark and it misleads the public as to the true place of origin, then registrations of trade mark is refused exofficio.

India enacted the geographical indications Act in 1999. If means an indication in relation to goods, which identifies such agricultural goods, natural goods, manufactured goods, any goods of handicrafts industry stuff a locality in that territory as the case may be, where a given quality, reputation and other characteristics of such goods is essentially attributable to its geographical origin.

F. **Protection of new plant variety:** Plant varieties and animal breeds are developed by years of scientifically well-planned and hard work. Article 27 section 3b has the following implications. It requires that microorganism, non biological process and microbial processes must be patented. Plant varieties must be protected by patents. The concept is based on the realization that if commercial plant breeding in to be encouraged for benefit of agriculture and society(Mishra,1999). India has now evolved a system has protection of plant varieties.

Management and benefit

IPR is acquired for anticipated profits on commercialization of the concerned intellectual property. This would involve the following activities.

* Transfer of intellectual property rights in such a way as to generate the maximum profits from an intellectual property.

* Establishment collaboration to facilitate commercialization of IPR.

* Monitoring the infringements of IPR and enforcing one's rights where necessary.

- Renewal of patents and design periodically in every country where they were granted.

- It increases and safeguards, intellectual and artistic creations.

- It promotes spread of new ideas and technologies quickly.

- It encourages breeders in their efforts by offering the incentive of a share in the profits from the varieties developed by him.

- It enables an access to varieties protected by PBR laws.

- It competition among plant breeding organizations and thereby, benefit farmers.

- Intellectual property regimes on their conformity with ethical and human rights principles.

- It will be also helpful in the conservation of literary biodiversity, biological resources and economic, social, cultural and industrial development.

Criticisms

- It is encourages monopolies activities.

- Intellectual property right situation becomes quite complicated to management. It is a costly, time taking affair and may act as a disincentive for research and development efforts, especially by small groups.

- Threat to food security.

- It will be adversely affect biological diversity and ecological balance.

- It is detrimental to the livelihood of the poor population especially in developing countries.

Importance

The intellectual property is present context in very important. The protection of intellectual property is also associated with the innovation, creativity, research, industry and development in the society. Thus development has direct connection with the security. The proper management of research in this environment is of prime importance and need to be given due to emphasis. Selection of suitable projects, structured methods for their implementation, measures for effective of suitable projects, progress, system for financing the projects in an organization and other related aspect are very important Suitable techniques for measurement of various Indices used in the process of managing technology and modality of implementation procedures such as technology forecasting are as important. IPRs assist the business in all spheres of development and strategies adopting in expanding the business. The explosive growth of recent techniques of environment such as the development of microprocessors, mass storage, graphics, video compression high broadband communication network and the increasing computer and use of the internet.

CONCLUSION

Human being are superior from other living creatures because they posses intellect. Creative genius of human being creates intellectual property, which in turn, when property exploited, can earn wealth. Since it is essentially a creation of mind, therefore, it is called intellectual property. Invention, industrial, designs, literary and artistic works, symbols used to promote commerce are some commonly know from of intellectual property. The intellectual property laws regulate the creation, use and exploitation of creative labor. This is a breach the law which protects some of the finer manifestations of human achievement. Human rights approach requires that type and level of protection afforded under any intellectual property regime directly facilitate and promote scientific progress in application and do so in a manner that will broadly benefit members of society on an individual, corporate and international level. If also implies a right of access to the benefit of social again on both an individual and collective level. Traditional goal and rational of intellectual property regime to provide in incentives and reword to inventors, researchers and authors have been replaced by a new emphasis on the protection of investment.

REFERENCES

1.   Alston, P. "The international covenant on economic, social and cultural rights." In manual on human rights reporting, U.N. Doc. HR/PUB/91/1(1991).

2.   Chawla, H. S.(2002). Introduction to plant biotechnology second edition. Oxford IBH Publishing Co. Pvt. Ltd. New Delhi.

3.   Dubey, R. C. and Maheshwari, D.K.(2005). A textbook of microbiology. S. Chand Company L.T.D. Ram nagar, New Delhi.

4.   Gupta, V.K. (1999). Basic concepts of IPRs and their management in R&D. In lecture notes on patents, technology information, forecasting and assessment council, New Delhi.

5.   Mishra, J.P. (1999). Biotechnology intellectual property rights. Yojana, may issue, p.p. 15-20.

6.   Sing, B. D. (2005). Biotechnology, Kalyani Publishers Ludhiana, New Delhi, Noida(U.P.)

Chapter-8

INTELLECTUAL PROPERTY RIGHTS IN INDIA

RAMAVTAR SHARMA & NEERAJ BHARDWAJ*

Department of Military Science, Govt. Science College, Gwalior (MP)
*Department of Military Science, Govt. College Alampur, Bhind (MP)

Intellectual property rights are the rights given to persons over the creations of their minds and give the creator an exclusive right over the use of his/her creation for a certain period of time. Intellectual Property Rights (IPR), very broadly, are rights granted to creators and owners of works that are results of human intellectual creativity. These works can be in the industrial, scientific, literary and artistic domains, which can be in the form of an invention, a manuscript, a suite of software , or a business name .

DEVELOPMENT OF INTELLECTUAL PROPERTY LAW IN INDIA

Intellectual Property Right (IPR) in India was imported from the west. The Indian Trade and Merchandise Marks Act 1884, was the first Indian Law regarding IPR. The first Indian Patent Law was enacted in 1856 followed by a series of Acts being passed. They are Indian Patents and Designs Act in 1911 and Indian Copyright Act in 1914. Indian Trade and Merchandise Marks Act and Indian Copyright Act have been replaced by Trade and Merchandise Marks Act 1958 and Copyright Act 1957 respectively.

Intellectual Property Rights and its Development in India

India, as a developing country, had a transition period of five years (with effect from 01 January, 1995) till January 01, 2000 to apply the provisions of the Agreement. An additional transition period of five years, i.e., till January 01, 2005, is also available for extending product patent protection to areas of technology not protected so far. This would be mainly in the areas of pharmaceuticals and agricultural chemicals.

1. Patents

Patent is an intellectual property right relating to inventions and it is the grant of exclusive rights, for a limited period, provided by the Government to the patentee, in exchange of full disclosure of his invention and excluding others, from making, using, selling, importing the patented product or processes producing that product for any purposes. The purpose of this system is to encourage inventions by highlighting their promotion and utilization so as to contribute to the development of industries, which in turn, contributes to the promotion of technological innovations and to the transfer and dissemination of technology. Under the system, Patents ensure property rights for the invention for which patent have been granted, which may be extremely valuable to an individual or a company.

Patents shall be available and patent rights enjoyable without discrimination as to the place of invention, the field of technology and whether products are imported or locally produced. The trends of patents during the last 25 years in India have their roots in the formulation and implementation of the Indian Patent Act 1970, which became effective from April 20, 1972. There was a strategic shift from the liberal features of the Indian Patents and Designs Act 1922 to the new regime which introduced restrictive changes related to patenting of inventions especially in the areas of chemicals, pharmaceuticals, agrochemicals and foods. The granting of patents for inventions claiming substances intended for use or capable of being used as, food, medicine or drug or all substances resulting from chemical processes was withdrawn. The conditions for compulsory licensing were also made fairly liberal including the introduction of the concept of "license of right" for patents related to drugs, pharmaceuticals and foods.

2. Copyright

The copy right ensures that computer programs will be protected as literary works under the Berne Convention and outlines how databases should be protected. It also expands international copyright rules to cover rental rights. Authors of computer programs and procedures of sound recordings must have the right to prohibit the commercial rental of their works to the public. A similar exclusive right applies to films where commercial rental has led to widespread copyright, affecting copyright-owners potential earnings from their films. The performers must also have the right to prevent unauthorized recording, reproduction and broadcast of live performances for not less than 50 years. Producers of sound recordings must have the right to prevent the unauthorized reproduction of recordings for a period of 50 years.India's copyright law, laid down in the Indian Copyright Act, 1957 as amended by Copyright (Amendment) Act, 1999, fully reflects the Berne Convention on Copyrights, to which India is aparty. Additionally, India is party to the Geneva Convention for the Protection of rights of Producers of Phonograms and to the Universal Copyright Convention. India is also an active member of the World Intellectual Property Organization (WIPO), Geneva and UNESCO. The copyright law has been amended periodically to keep pace with changing requirements. The recent amendment to the copyright law, which came into force in May 1995, has ushered in comprehensive changes and brought the copyright law in line with the developments in satellite broadcasting, computer software and digital technology. The amended law has made provisions for the first time, to protect performer's rights as envisaged in the Rome Convention. Several measures have been adopted to strengthen and streamline the enforcement of copyrights. These include the setting up of a Copyright Enforcement Advisory Council, training programmes for enforcement officers and setting up of special policy cells to deal with cases relating to infringement of copyrights.

3. Trademark

Trade marks have been defined as any sign, or any combination of signs capable of distinguishing the goods or services of one undertaking from those of other undertakings. Such distinguishing marks constitute protectable subject matter. The Agreement provides that initial registration and each renewal of registration shall be for a term of not less than 7 years and the registration shall be renewable indefinitely. Compulsory licensing of trade marks is not permitted.

Keeping in view the changes in trade and commercial practices, globalization of trade, need for simplification and harmonization of trade marks registration systems etc., A comprehensive review of the Trade and Merchandise Marks Act, 1958 was made and a Bill to repeal and replace the 1958 Act has since been passed by Parliament and notified in the Gazette on December 30, 1999.

This Act not only makes Trade Marks Law, TRIPS compatible but also harmonizes it with international systems and practices. Work is underway to bring the law into force.

4. Geographical Indications

Geographical indications of goods are defined as that aspect of industrial property, which adverts to the geographical indication referring to a country or to a place, situated there is as being the country or place or origin of that product. The given product should have a specific geographical origin and posse's qualities or a reputation due to that place of origin. A place name is sometimes used to identify a product. This geographical indication not only refers to where the product was made, but more importantly, it identifies the product's special characteristics which are the result of the products origin. Using the place name when the product was made elsewhere or when it doesn't have the usual characteristics can mislead consumers, and it can lead to unfair competition. Some exceptions are allowed, for example if the name is already protected as a trademark or if it has become a generic term.

5. Industrial Design

An industrial design is that aspect of a useful article, which is ornamental or aesthetic. It may consist of three-dimensional features such as the shape or surface of the article, or two dimensional features such as patterns, lines or color.

Industrial design is applied to a wide variety of products of industry or handicraft; from watches, jewellery, fashion and other luxury items to industrial and medical implements; from house ware, furniture and electrical appliances to vehicles and architectural structures, from practical goods and textile designs to leisure items, such as toys and pet accessories. A new designs law repealing and replacing the

Designs Act, 1911 has been passed by Parliament in the Budget Session, 2000. This Act has been brought into force from May 11, 2001.

6. Layout Designs of Integrated Circuits

A "layout-design (topography)" is defined as the three dimensional disposition, however expressed, of the elements, at least one of which is an active element, and of some or all of the interconnections of an integrated circuit, or such a three dimensional disposition prepared for an integrated circuit intended for manufacture. The obligation to protect layout-designs applies to such layout-designs that are original in the sense that they are the result of their creators own intellectual effort and are not commonplace among creators of layout-designs and manufacturers of integrated circuits at the time of their creation. The exclusive rights include the right of reproduction and the right of importation, sale and other distribution for commercial purposes.

7. Protection of undisclosed information

The protection must apply to information that is secret, which has commercial value because it is a secret and that has been subject to reasonable steps to keep it a secret. That does not require undisclosed information to be treated as a form of property, but it does require that a person lawfully in control of such information must have the possibility of preventing it from being disclosed to, acquired by, or used by others without his/her consent in a manner contrary to honest commercial practices. "Manner contrary to honest commercial practices" includes breach of contract, breach of confidence and inducement to breach, as well as the acquisition of undisclosed information by third parties who knew, or were grossly negligent in failing to know, that such practices were involved in the acquisition.

8. Plant Varieties

The protection of new plant varieties is another aspect of intellectual property rights, and as such seeks to acknowledge the achievements of breeders of new plant varieties by giving them, for a limited period, an exclusive right. To obtain such protection, the new varieties must satisfy specific criteria. Variety is defined as a plant grouping within a single botanical taxon of the lowest known rank. Provided that the herb should be new or novel, distinct, uniform, stable and have a satisfactory denomination. The organization overseeing the protection of new plant varieties is referred to as UPOV (The International Union for the Protection of New Varieties of Plants.

CONCLUSION

IPR are considered to achieve economic, social and technological advancement that protects the ideas and stimulates innovation, design and helps to the creation of technology. The various types of IPR were designed to provide the formal basis of ownership of developed knowledge with benefit sharing between partners in innovation to create a niche of themselves. It also leads to wealth creation. The function of IPR regime is also to facilitate the transfer of technology in the form of joint ventures and licensing. The social purpose of IPR is to provide protection for the results of investment in the development of new technology, thus giving the incentive and means of finance for further research and development of knowledge base; while basic social objective of IPR protection is that the exclusive rights given to the inventor, aimed at fine tuning the balance that has to be formed between the legitimate interests of rights holders.

REFERENCES

1. www.wipo.int

2. Ganguli P. Indian Path towards TRIPS compliance. World Patent Information, 2003; 25: 143.

3. www.iprlawindia.org

4. http://en.wikipedia.org/wiki/General_Agreement_on_Tariffs_and_Trade

5. http://en.wikipedia.org/wiki United_Nations_Conference_on_Trade_and_Development

6. http://en.wikipedia.org/wiki/ United_Nations_Commission_on_International_Trade_Law

7. Ganguli P. Intellectual Property Rights in transition. World Patent Information, 1998; 20: 171.

8. Ganguli P. Intellectual Property Rights - unleashing the knowledge economy, New Delhi, India. Tata McGraw Hill; 2001. ISBN 0-07-463860.

9. Ganguli P. Intellectual Property Rights. Imperatives for the knowledge industry. World Patent Information, 2000; 22: 167.

10. Ganguli P. Patents and Patent information in 1979 and 2004: a perspective from India. World Patent Information, 2004; 26: 61.

11. Lall S. Indicators of the relative importance of IPRs in developing countries., Research Policy, 2003; 32: 1657.

12. Narayananan P. In: Patent Law, 2nd ed, Eastern Law House, 1997.

13. The Patents Act 1970, Universal Law Publishing Co. Pvt. Ltd, 2005.p. 6-31, 42-45.

14. Ramakrishna T. In: Basic Principles and Acquistation of IPR. CIPRA, NLSIU, Bangalore, 2005.

Chapter-9

INTELLECTUAL PROPERTY RIGHTS & THEIR IMPORTANCE IN RESEARCH, BUSINESS AND INDUSTRY

K. S. SENGAR, SUBHASH CHAND AND CHAITANYA KUMAR GOYAL

Govt. P. G. College, Sheopur (M P)

The term IPRs refers to any ideas innovative invention & creative expression for which exclusive rights are recognized. IPRs play a very important role in the economy of nation. IPRs can open the door to new revenue streams through licensing, copyrights, patents, trademark and trade secrets. In the era of globalization, the importance of IPRs has increased manifolds in all fields of technology.

Intellectual Property Rights may be defined as any thought, ideas, innovative invention and creative expression for which exclusive rights are recognized. Common types of IPR include trademark, Patent Copyrights and trade secret. It provide rights to the inventor or creator of that property through which He/She can reap commercial and other benefits from their creative and innovative work.

The base of these laws and administrative procedures of IPR have been first come in Europe. The trends of awarding patent began during the 14th century. In India patent laws were much recently observed, in 1856 the first act was established based on British patent system. There is extensive international system for defining, protecting and enforcing intellectual property rights comprising both multilateral treaty schemes and international organizations include the Trade Related Aspects of Intellectual Property Rights (TRIPS), World Intellectual Property Organization (WIPO), World Custom Organization(WCO), United Nations Commission On International Trade Organization (UNCITRAL), World Trade Organization (WTO), European Organization (EU). Nonetheless there are variation in the respect and enforcement of rights at a local level.

IP plays an important role in the modern economy. IPRs is a strong tool which protects investment, time, money & efforts which were invested by the creator of an idea/product, as IPRs grants the creator/innovator an exclusive right to fully utilize this creation. This results in the economic development by promoting a healthy environment towards new ideas and creation. IPRs contributes enormously to our national economies. Some industries across our economy rely on the adequate enforcement of their patents, trademark and copy rights while consumer use IP to ensure they bought safe guaranteed products.

Intellectual property rights create high paying jobs drives economic growth of country. The importance of intellectual property rights for international trade and commerce has been recognized by the whole world. The use of the IP by the society brings about social, economical & industrial prosperity in the country.

In the era of globalization the abundant supply of goods and services on the market has made very challenging for any business whether it is small or big. In this era ahead of competitors in this environment, every business strives to create new and improved products offered by the competitor. To differentiate for their success in today's markets businesses rely on innovation that reduce the production cost and/ or improve the quality product. All businesses, especially those which are successful, nowadays depend on the effective use of different type of IPRs to obtain benefit and maintain a substantial competitive edge in the market place. IPRs provide a basis for businesses to prevent others from copying their products or using their innovation and create a strong brand identity by product differentiation through the strategic use of one and other type of IPRs.

It is very well known that the role of IPR has increased at an unprecedented pace during the last two decade. There has been a dramatic change in the demand for patent, trademark, copyrights and other different types of registered rights. In this process IP rights have been modified or new provision have been created in order to cover new areas of science and technology such as IT (Information technology), Biotechnology and now different types of service sector are included in it.

An efficient and equitable intellectual property system can help all countries to realize intellectual property's potential as a catalyst for economic development and social and cultural well being. The IPR system helps strike a balance between the interests of innovators and the public interest, providing an environment in which creativity and invention can flourish, for the benefit of all.

Research in Biotechnology, IT (Information Technology) field is very expensive, time consuming and unpredictable in nature. The outcomes of these researches that has some commercial value. In this era of competition global IP standard has become mandatory for the companies to get back benefits on heavy investment made in R&D and business development.

CONCLUSION

In this fast growing world it has become imperative for every researcher to gain basic knowledge of IPRs. It is essential for the economic growth of the industries that the innovative outcome of the research shall be protected under the IPRs. By the judicial use of IPRs heavy investment poured in research and business activities can be regained. The use of the IP by the society brings about social, economical, industrial & cultural prosperity in the country where such rights are granted.

REFERENCES

1. www.icai.org/resource_file/19893725-732.pdf

2. ip.india.nic.in

3. http://www.wipo.int/export/sites/www/freepublications/en/intproperty/450/

4. http://en.wikipedia.org/wiki/Intellectual_property

5. http://www.ncbi.nlm.nih.gov/pmc/articles/PMC3217699/

6. http://www.unido.org/fileadmin/user_media/Publications/Research_and_statist

7. http://www.jli.edu.in/blog/intellectual-property-rights-iprs-and-its-importance

8. http://tmroe.com/blog/intellectual-property-and-its-importance-in-modern-business

9. http://gipcdev.blackbarn.net/sites/default/files/documents/iparguments.pdf

10. http://www.theglobalipcenter.com/why-are-intellectual-property-rights-important

Chapter-10

INTELLECTUAL PROPERTY RIGHTS & THEIR IMPORTANCE IN RESEARCH, BUSINESS AND INDUSTRY

BASUKI NATH DUBEY

Mahatama Gandhi College of Law, Gwalior (MP)

The Intellectual Property in present context is very important. The Intellectual Property is an intangible thing but having value both in the real world as well as in the electronic environment. The protection of Intellectual Property is also associated with the innovation, creativity, and research and development in the society, as without proper protection of these things, it will be doomed. If there is constant threat to the Intellectual Property, person cannot provide attention to other things. Thus inventions, discoveries and new ideas will not come out unless the inventor feels that these will benefit him in future. Thus development has direct connection with the security. If a person loses faith in the political community and political community fails to assure him about the safety and security of his property in general and Intellectual Property in particular, he will not devote himself for developmental work.

Creation, enjoyment and accumulation of 'property' has been a central activity of human life. Out of four objects of human life, i.e., Artha, Kama, Dharma and Moksha the first object is i.e., money. It is a fundamental requirement of sustaining material life.

According to Halsbury's Laws of England[1] property is that which belongs to a person exclusively of others and can be subject to bargain and sale. It includes goodwill, trademarks, licences to use a patent, book debts, options to purchase, life policies and other rights under a contract.

---

[1]3rd Ed. Vol. 33, p. 310

Property can be classified into two broad categories:

(i)   Tangible - (Movable and Immovable)

(ii)   Intangible - (Intellectual Property)

Meaning of Intellectual Property

Human being is superior from other living creatures because they possess intellect. Creative genius of human being creates intellectual property; which in turn, when properly exploited, can earn wealth. Since it is essentially a creation of mind, therefore, it is called intellectual property: inventions, industrial designs, literary and artistic works, symbols used to promote commerce are some commonly known forms of intellectual property.

Why Legal Protection for Intellectual Property

Every human Endeavour which promotes economic, social, scientific and cultural development of society must be encouraged and the creator must be suitably rewarded by affording legal protection to his intellectual creation. Thus the intellectual Property Right (IPRs) are the legal rights governing the use of creations of human minds.

The intellectual property laws regulate the creation, use and exploitation of mental or creative labour. It prevents third parties from becoming unjustly enriched by reaping what they have not sown. This is a branch of the law which protects some of the finer manifestations of human achievement.[2]

Scope of Intellectual Property Rights

The Convention establishing World Intellectual Property Organisation (WIPO) has given a wider definition of IPRs. According to this definition the IPRs shall include the rights relating to:

(i)   Literary, artistic and scientific work;

(ii)   Performances of performing artists, phonograms and broadcasts;

(iii) Inventions in all fields of human Endeavour;

(iv)   Scientific designs;

(v)   Trade Marks, service marks, and commercial names and designations;

(vi)   Protection against unfair competition and; all other rights resulting from intellectual activity in the industrial, scientific literary or artistic fields.

Intellectual Property

"Intellectual Property" is an intellectual work, produced by the intellect of human brain. For example, literary work produced by the authors, musical work produced by the musicians, inventions invented by the inventors, coining of trade marks used in the course of business or trade, design of industrial products, etc. are intellectual properties as they are created by the human intellect. Computer programming is also an intellectual property as it is also the creation of human intellect. The person who

---

[2]W.R. Cornish, Intellectual Property,. 3rd Ed., 2001 Universal Law Publishing Delhi, p. 3.

creates an intellectual piece of work owns it like any other tangible property like land or movable goods. "Intellectual property" like tangible property is owned by its owner to the exclusion of all others. The owner of intellectual property has exclusive right over his intellectual property. No one can make use of intellectual property without the consent of the owner of the intellectual property. For example, no one can copy literary, musical piece of work, work an invention or apply a design to and industrial product without the consent of the author, musician, or the inventor, as the case may be, who has created this piece of creative work. Similarly, no one can make use of the trade marks without the consent of its proprietor. However the owner of intellectual property may assign intellectual property itself or any interest in the intellectual property in the favour of any other person in consideration of monetary gain. For example, an author may assign the copyright in his literary work in the favour of any other person in consideration of lump sum amount of royalty. Similarly, a musician may assign a composition composed by him to any other person in consideration of monetary gain. Similarly, an inventor may assign his invention or grant a licence to work his invention in the favour of any other person in consideration of commercial gain to him.

Thus, a person enjoys exclusive rights with respect to his intellectual property which he has created by the intellect of his brain.

Intellectual property law

The exclusive rights which a person enjoys with respect to his intellectual property are his 'intellectual property rights' (hereinafter referred to as IPRs). The law that protects the 'intellectual property rights' is known as intellectual property law. For example, copyright law protects the copyright of authorize, musicians, etc. with respect to literary or musical work, etc. The law of patents protects the inventions of the inventors. The law of trade marks protects the trade marks used in the course of trade by the traders or businessmen for their goods or services.

According to agreement on Trade Related Intellectual Property Rights (TRIPs) agreement between the members of the World Trade Organisation (WTO) F-2 intellectual property law includes law relating to;

1. Copyright and related rights;

2. Trade marks, trade names and service marks;

3. Geographical indications;

4. Industrial Designs;

5. Patents;

6. Layout Designs of Integrated Circuits;

7. Undisclosed Information.

Intellectual Property Law at International Level

Law relating to intellectual property may be divided under the following two heads:-

(i) Intellectual property law relating to industrial property; and

(ii)   Intellectual property law relating to copyright.

i. Intellectual Property law relating to industrial property : The significance of intellectual property right in the international trade had been realized as early as in the 19th century. As in 1883 an international convention on the protection of industrial property was convened in Paris with the efforts of inventors and industrialists. Originally the Paris Convention was signed by representatives of eleven countries, on March 20, 1883 which became effective on 7th march, 1884. This convention known as "Paris Industrial Property Convention, 1883" took within its fold the Patents, Trade Marks, Designs but did not deal with the Copyrights. The first international convention an copyright was the Berne Convention of 1886.

Paris convention

The convention known as **"Paris Industrial Property Convention, 1883"** took within its fold the Patents, Trade Marks, Designs, etc.

Article 1(1) of the Paris Convention provides as follows:

"The countries to which this convention applies constitute a Union for the protection of industrial property."

The protection of industrial property has its object patents, utility models, industrial designs, trade marks, service marks, trade names indication of source or origin and the repression of unfair competition.

The Member States of Paris convention guaranteed the nationals of each Member state the same treatment as was given to their own nationals. The Paris Convention was revised a number of times. It was revised in 1900 in Brussels, in Brussels, in 1911 in Hague in 1925 in Washington, in 1934 in London, in 1958 in Lisbon, and in the last in 1967 in Stockholm.

India deposited its instrument of accession to the Paris Convention for the protection of industrial property on 7th September, 1998 and became member of the Paris Convention with effect from 7th December, 1998.

Important features of Paris Convention

Important features of the "Paris Industrial Property Convention, 1883" are as follows :

1. Protection of Industrial Property

The Paris Convention aims at protecting the intellectual property relating to industrial property. For example, Paris Convention took within its fold the Patents, Trade Marks, Designs.

Article 1(1) of the Paris Convention provides as follows:

"The countries to which this Convention applies constitute a Union for the protection of industrial property."

The protection of industrial property has its object patents, utility models. Industrial designs, trade marks, service marks, trade names, indication of source or origin and the repression of unfair competition.

2. Intellectual Property Law relating to copyright

Two important conventions relating to intellectual property law relating to copyright are:

(i)   Bern Convention, 1886; and

(ii)   Universal Copyright Convention, 1952 as revised in 1971.

Role of Intellectual property law in the economic development

Intellectual property law has been developed to protect the intellectual property. As has already been explained intellectual property is the creation of the intellect of human brain. Literary work, music compositions, inventions, creation of designs, coining of trade marks, etc. are the examples of intellectual property created by the intellect of human brain.

Intellectual property has immense economic value when it is put into practice and has the capability of effecting the market also. Industrial revolution in the human history is one such example. Machines invented by the intellect of human brain caused the mass production of the goods din short period of time and created a situation where supply exceeded the demand for the goods. Such situation effected the economies of the nations where the industrial revolution took place. As a matter of fact economic development of any nation is directly related to its industrial development. Whereas industrial development itself depends upon the inventions invented by the intellect of human brain. Inventions as intellectual properties are protected by the Intellectual Property Law. Protection of intellectual property rights under the Intellectual Property in the form of literary work, inventions, coining of trade marks, industrial designs, etc., and disclose it to the public for the benefit of the society.

The intellectual property law confers upon the creator of intellectual property an exclusive right with respect to his intellectual property for a specified period. This exclusive right of the creator over his intellectual property includes his right to assign his intellectual property, or without assigning his intellectual property itself, transfer any interest in his intellectual property in the favour of any other person in consideration of monetary gain.

To prevent the unauthorized use of the intellectual property without the consent of the owner of the intellectual property law provides for the remedies in the form of: (i) injunctions, (ii) damages, and (iii) accounts of profits in the favour of the owner of intellectual property against those who make an unauthorized use of his intellectual property right without his permission. Such provision under the intellectual property law protects the commercial interest of person in his intellectual property.

Protection of commercial interest of the owners of the intellectual property law encourages the inventors, authors, musicians, creators of designs of industrial products, etc. to disclose their creations to the public without any fear of the infringement of their creations by others. Protection of intellectual property right of the inventors over their inventions by intellectual property law not only protects the economic interest of the inventors but also the economic interest of the nation to which these owners of intellectual properties belong.

By protecting the economic interest of the owner of the intellectual property, intellectual property law encourages the inventors to invent new inventions, create new designs for industrial products, which are crucial to the economic development of any nation.

Intellectual property law has become more important in the recent past due to an unprecedented development in the field of science and technology particularly in the field of information technology. In the age of satellites and internet, any development that takes place in one corner of the world gets communicated to the other corner in no time. This gives rise to enormous possibility of unauthroised working of inventions or piracy of industrial deigns, infringement or passing off the trade marks, etc. at the international level. In such situation rights of a person with property law. Because unauthorized working of inventions or piracy of industrial designs affects adversely not only the individual commercial interest of the owner of the intellectual property, but also affects the economy of a nation to which the downer of intellectual property belongs.

But stringent intellectual property law to protect the interest of the owners of the intellectual property does not mean grant of perpetual exclusive rights to the owner of the intellectual property in total disregard of the public interest.

TRIPs agreement aims at balancing the interests of various stakeholders, including innovators, producers and consumers in a manner that enhances, "social and economic welfare." As Article 7 of the TRIPs agreement provides as follows:

"The protection and enforcement of intellectual property rights should contribute to the promotion of technological innovation and to the transfer and dissemination of technology, to the mutual advantage of producers and user of technological knowledge and in manner conducive to a social and economic welfare and to a balance of rights and obligations."

"Copyright" is an 'exclusive right' exercised over a work produced by the intellectual labour of a person. As a in **Sulmanglam R. Jayalakshmi V. Meta Musical**[3], the Madras High court held that "the right which a person acquires in his literary or artistic work which is the result of his intellectual labour is called his "copyright"."

'Copyright' is not restricted to literary or artistic work. '"Copyright" applies to different other kinds of works also like dramatic, musical, cinematographic film, computer programme, work of architecture and sound recording and any other worked which is produced by the intellectual labour of a person. In other words, As the subject-matter of copyright is the work produced by the intellectual labour of a person therefore, the right to "copyright" is a right to "intellectual property of a person."

REFERENCES

1.   Bhadwani, M.K., Law relating to Intellectual Property Rights, CLP.

2.   Paul, Meenu, Intellectual Property Law. ALA.

3.   Nyayadeep Vol. -XII issue Jan. 2011.

Chapter-11

ROLE OF IPR IN AGRICULTURE BIOTECHNOLOGY

SAROJ SHRIVASTAVA AND SARITA SHRIVASTAVA*

Department of Economics, Sarojini Naidu Govt. Girls P. G. College, Bhopal.
*Department of Zoology, Govt. Model Science College, Gwalior

In past few years, agriculture in most of the developing countries has been getting exposed to an entirely new set of technologies, the developments in the area of biotechnology in particular. This frontier technology becomes particularly important in developing country's agriculture with stagnating productivity growth and crops confronting many biotic and abiotic stresses. The constraints on productivity in developing country agriculture have become much more acute since late eighties, when green revolution varieties reached their maximum yield potential. The advancements in biotechnology seem to offer, a way out, of this impasse by opening an opportunity to attain higher productivity with sustainable development of agriculture in these countries. The developments in biotechnology, however, have been accompanied by a stronger intellectual property rights (IPR) regime. In fact, with the advancements in this technology, stronger instruments are being used for the protection of technology, which are highly exclusionist in their approach. This may pose severe challenges for the developing countries as advances in this technology are largely in the private sector and these new trends in the IPR regime seems to foreclose the entry of public sector in this domain. This is happening despite of the fact that a large number of developing countries have agreed to a relatively newer IPR regime at the WTO forum. In fact, coverage of agricultural sector through an IPR regime is a recent phenomenon in the developing countries.

In this context, several issues pertaining to the role of government and space for public sector supported R&D in agriculture have been raised. The dynamism with which countries develop and use new technologies defines their paths of technological development.

This dynamism reflects on the cumulative pattern of production and skills acquired over time and sketches out their technological trajectories. Thus one idea has been that public sector R&D institutions should develop more strength and competence in the realm of the frontier technologies. Thus the emergence of biotechnology is also accompanied by an intense debate on techno-globalization vis-a-vis the role of nation-state in technological development. The increasing role of knowledge in agricultural production and the growing challenge of environment management in particular has to be acknowledged. A broad range of agricultural genetic diversity needs to be available and utilized in order to feed this growing population (Lidderan and Sonnino, 2012).

BIOTECHNOLOGY- A PANACEA FOR GROWTH!

The Convention on Biological Diversity (CBD), 1992, defined biotechnology as, "any technological application that uses biological systems, living organisms or derivatives thereof, to make or modify products or processes for specific uses." This technology facilitates plant breeders to monitor the outcomes of conventional crossings and selection, allow useful genes to be identified and cloned and make it possible for genes from the same species to be utilized more quickly and precisely than do the methods of traditional plant breeding. But most attention now is focused on transfer of genes between different species only, transgenic crops are often called as GMOs. Though the scope of plant biotechnology is very wide, now the attention is on transfer of genes between different species to develop transgenic crops. Tissue culture techniques are of great interest for the collection, multiplication and storage of plant germplasm (Bunn et al., 2007).

ADVANTAGES OF BIOTECHNOLOGY

1. Cost-Reduction

The Bt cotton variety contains a foreign gene obtained from Bacillus thuringiensis. This bacterial gene, introduced genetically into the cotton seeds, protects the plants from bollworm (A. lepidoptora), a major pest of cotton. The worm feeding on the leaves of a BT cotton plant becomes lethargic and sleepy, thereby causing less damage to the plant. Field trials have shown that farmers in China who grew the Bt variety obtained 25%-75% more cotton than those who grew the normal variety.

Also, Bt cotton requires only two sprays of chemical pesticide against eight sprays for normal variety. According to the director general of the Indian Council of Agricultural Research, India uses about half of its pesticides on cotton to fight the bollworm menace.

2. Yield Enhancement

Biotechnology offers several ways by which average yields can be directly increased. One is through improvements in the "architecture" of the plant to enable it to absorb more photosynthetic energy or convert a larger portion of mat energy into grain rather than stem or leaf. Another approach, for climates where this is useful, is to modify the plant for a shorter growing season by enhancing its efficiency in the use of fertilizer, pesticides and water (Y. D. Tyagi, 1985).

3. Improves Nutritional Values

There are many possibilities by which biotechnology improves the nutritional value of cereals by enhancing the presence of special nutrients or chemicals. A commercial example is the increase in the levels of biotin (vitamin H) for application in animal and human nutrition.

Biotechnology has been targeted at rice and tried used to improve upon rice to meet the Vitamin A and iron deficiencies. New varieties of transgenic maize that contain higher oil levels to boost energy and improve feeding efficiency or have characteristics to reduce phosphorus in animal waste are examples that are currently under development. In an interesting development, that is, certainly relevant to feed grains, is a patent covering the insertion of a protein into plants, when eaten would facilitate control of animal parasites.

DIFFICULTIES OF BIOTECHNOLOGY

1. Implications in monopolisation

Social, economic and ecological impacts of monopolization of agriculture are serious. The domination of few HYV'S and a handful of crop species have spurred the so called green revolution, fuelled by heavy inputs of irrigation, chemical fertilizers and pesticides. Its gains are likely to be only short term while its deleterious impacts are agrobiodiversity, soil fertility and hydrological cycle would persist much longer. For instance, in Dhikonia village in Baran district of Rajasthan the local farmers complain that wheat hybrid today yields only one third of what they used to get from traditional varieties from katya, which they replaced at the instance of local agricultural officers. The traditional varieties neither are easily available today nor perform well given the drastically impoverished soil and water regimes over the last two decades. The farmers in northern Andhra Pradesh similarly found themselves doomed due to the poor quality pesticides on them by the private companies in collusion with bureaucrats. The monoculture of cotton spread all over the landscape made it more susceptible to pest attack. The resultant crop failure was unprecedented causing loss beyond recovery and forcing farmers to commit suicide. The challenge before us is to promote appropriate technology, both within and outside the IPR framework, through a variety of institutions, public as well as private.

2. Constraints on Public Research

The agricultural sector in the developing countries is passing through a difficult phase. The challenges range from the post-green revolution stagnation in primary agricultural crops to large-scale malnutrition and declining R&D allocations. One of the major constraints agriculture is facing in most of the developing countries relates to farm productivity. Green revolution contributed to achieving higher yields. The relevance of this technology for developing countries has to be seen in the light of two factors. The first pertains to the priorities that agro-biotech research has seen thus far, and the second relates to the possibilities of access of small farmers to this technology. The location-specific dimension, while working out any strategy for R&D support demands that it should have involvement of the local resources as local knowledge and local biodiversity. This approach only would provide a sustainable agricultural system (K. Raj, 2002).

IPR IN THE FIELD OF BIOTECHNOLOGY FOR FOOD AND AGRICULTURE

Agricultural biotechnology involves scientific methods that create, improve or modify plants and animals. This technology allows scientists to move desirable genes from one plant to another or from one animal to another. Through agricultural biotechnology, researchers transfer desirable genes (insect resistance, large muscle mass, better flavor, longer shelf life) into various plants and/or animals.

In 1980, the United States Supreme Court made a landmark decision in the Diamond versus Chakrabarty case. The ruling stated that a live, human-made, genetically engineered bacterium (of the genus Pseudomonas, that was modified to break down components of crude oil) could be patented, thus initiating an era of massive private investment in biotechnology and of rapid expansion in the patenting of new biotechnological innovations and products. Many biotechnology companies and universities have since applied for and been granted patents on a wide range of biotechnology processes and products, involving genes, viruses, bacteria and even living higher organisms.

CONCERNS HAVE BEEN RAISED REGARDING THE FOLLOWING ISSUES

a) The limits of patentability - The difference between invention and discovery becomes a matter of interpretation when it refers to living material. The isolation of a gene from its natural environment and the identification of its function render the gene and its sequence an invention for patenting purposes in some countries.

b) Patenting of "enabling technologies" (i.e. technologies that are essential for the practical implementation of a wide range of other biotechnological processes and products) -This issue is of great importance as it has an impact on access to these technologies, not only by developing countries but also by the agricultural research system in general.

c) The multiplicity of patents required to develop an agricultural product - Developments in modern agricultural biotechnology require the use of several processes and products, which in most cases will be subject to patent protection.

d) Patents on specific genes usually extend to the genetically modified organisms (GMO) into which the genes are inserted, thus bringing the entire organism under patent protection. This question has raised considerable debate in the crop sector.

e) Concentration of the agricultural industry - Another important element is that a small number of multinational companies (MNCs) dominate the field of agricultural biotechnology. Companies from developed countries therefore own many of the important IPRs in this area, and the power that this provides is concentrated in very few hands. For example, it is reported that of the roughly 270 patents related to genes of the soil bacterium *Bacillus thuringiensis (Bt)* granted from 1986 'to 1997 in countries of the Organisation for Economic Co-operation and Development (OECD), about 60% were owned by only six MNCs.

The impact of IPRs on agricultural biotechnology in developing countries was quite substantial. Some of the potential consequences mentioned are:

a)   Increased dependency of developing countries on developed countries: -That the existence of strong IPRs, and the fact that the rights over the technologies and products are often owned by MNCs, might lead to (increased) dependence by developing country farmers on MNCs and developed countries.

b)   Patenting of genetic resources native to developing countries: -Patents can and have been issued to companies from developed countries over genetic material from developing countries, particularly for pharmaceutical and cosmetic purposes. In some cases, the lack of appropriate mechanisms for sharing of benefits has generated considerable controversy.

LEGAL PERSPECTIVE

AGRICULTURAL BIOTECHNOLOGY: UNITED STATES STATUTORY LAW

The three types of patent and patent-like protection available in the United States for living material: utility patents, Plant Variety Protection Act (PVPA) certificates, and plant patents. A utility patent, as would be obtained for an ordinary invention, provides the greatest protection but is typically more difficult and expensive to obtain. The plant patent and PVPA certificate provide attractive alternatives to inventors and breeders. Plant patents are designed to protect asexually reproduced plants. PVPA certificates are not patents at all, and are administered by the U.S. Department of Agriculture to protect sexually reproduced plants.

CONVENTION ON BIOLOGICAL DIVERSITY

CBD came into effect in 1993 and was signed by 171 countries till date (CBD 1999). The convention reflects the worldwide concern to prevent unfair exploitation of the rich genetic wealth and traditional knowledge of the developing countries by the developed world. CBD reaffirms sovereign rights of the member nations over their genetic resources. It requires all the nations to facilitate global access to their genetic resources; but stipulates that such access must be on the basis of prior informed consent (PIC) of the country of origin. The terms of the agreement could include sharing of benefits, technology transfer and preferential location of research and development units of country of origin. It also require member countries to obtain traditional knowledge of sustainable uses only with the approval of its holders, their involvement in its wider application and sharing the resulting benefits with them. It requires nations to protect the traditional knowledge and customary practices relating to uses of biological resources.

NATIONAL SCENARIO

Commercial interests in the new developments in biotechnology led to pressure being exerted on WTO member states to provide better patent protection in this area. The text of Article 27.3(b) is the result of the attempt by certain Northern countries and the biotechnology lobby to impose private, monopolistic rights over biological resources. Article 27.3(b) represents a major new development in IPR law; since it blurs the distinction between "inventions", which are patentable under traditional patent law, and "discoveries", which are not. The majority of the developing countries, during the TRIPs negotiations, objected to the notion of the patentability of biological resources.

TRIPs is the first international instrument to require IPR protection for life forms, however the obligation at present is limited to microorganisms and plant varieties. The TRIPs member states are under an obligation to implement Art 27.3(b) either through patents or effective sui generis system, with the least developing countries to develop such system by 2005. There is, however, a clause under Article 27.2 which makes allowances for patent exclusions where necessary to protect "...human, animal or plant life or health or to avoid serious prejudice to the environment..." There have been attempts to redress the imbalance between plant breeder's rights versus farmers' rights. Capitalising on the TRIPS flexibility to adopt the sui generis system for PVP and maintaining a balance between the rights of farmers and breeders, India has formulated fanner friendly plant variety protection (PVP) laws. **The Protection of Plant Varieties and Farmers Rights Act, 2001 of India** , for the very first time, put in place a law togrant Breeder's Rights on new varieties of seeds as well as grants Farmers rights.The other related Acts include the Patents Act, 1970; the Geographical Indications (Registration and Protection) Act, 1999; the Biological Diversity Act, 2002; the Environmental protection Act, 1986; and the Seeds Act 1966. The Patent Act 1970, amended twice in 1999 and 2002, is in harmony with the TRIPS Agreement. Product patent on genes however remains a gruyere.

The Protection of Plant Varieties and Farmers' Rights Act, 2001, hailed as progressive and pro-developing countries legislation provides for well-defined Breeder's rights as well as strong and proactive Farmers' rights. Its intent is the establishment of an effective system for protection of plant varieties, the rights of farmers and plant breeders and to encourage the development of new varieties of plants. The Act recognises the necessity of protecting the rights of farmers in respect of their contribution made in conserving, improving and making available plant genetic resources for the development of new plant varieties. In addition, there are clauses to protect the rights of researchers as well as public interest. The Indian law actually grants very restricted rights to researchers because of the acknowledgement of Essentially Driven Varieties (EDV) for which breeder's authorisation is needed. To secure public interest, certain varieties may not be registered if it is felt that prevention of commercial exploitation of such variety is necessary to "protect order or public morality or human, animal and plant life and health or to avoid serious prejudice to environment." The Act also provides for the granting of compulsory license to a party other than the Breeder if it is shown that the reasonable requirements for seeds have not been satisfied or that the seed of the variety is not available to the public at a reasonable price. The Indian legislation is the first in the world to grant formal rights to farmers in a way that their self-reliance is not jeopardized.

However, the amendments in Patent Act create a new scenario. The 2nd Amendment makes changes in the definition of what is not an invention. This has opened the floodgates for the patenting of genetically engineered seeds.

According to Section 3(i) of the Indian Patent Act, the following is not an invention: "Any process for the medical, surgical, creative, prophylactic or other treatment of human beings or any process for a similar treatment of animals or plants or render them free of disease or to increase their economic value or that of their products."

In the 2nd Amendment however, the mention of "plants" have been deleted from this section. This deletion implies that a method or process modification of a plant can now be counted as an invention and therefore can be patented. Thus the exclusive rights associated with patents can now cover the method of producing Bt. cotton by introducing genes of a bacterium Bacilus thurengerisis in cotton to produce toxins to kill the bollworm. In other words, Monsanto can now have *Bt.* cotton patents in India.

The Patent Act has also added a new section 3(j). This section allows for the production or propagation of genetically engineered plants to count as an invention. Its status as an invention thus deems it. But this section excludes as inventions "plants and animals include seeds, varieties and species and essentially biological processes for production or propagation of plants and animals". Since plants produced through the use of new biotechnologies are not technically considered "essentially biological," section 3(j) has found another way to create room for Agribiotech companies. This loophole, couched in the guise of scientific advancement, thus allows patents on GMOs and hence opens the floodgate for patenting transgenic plants. What is most concerning is how the language of section 3(j) is a verbatim translation into India law of Article 27.3 (b) of TRIPS Agreement. While, Art 27.3(b) is under review, the Indian government should have insisted on the completion of the review instead of changing India's Patent Law (Wadhera, 2000).

While having already an explicit law providing protection on plant varieties in the form of Protection of Plant Varieties and Farmers' Rights Act, 2001, what was the need to provide product patents on seeds through amendment of the Patent Act? It creates confusion, as it does not make clear which protection shall be granted to seeds of Genetically Modified crops. Shall they be patented or shall they be protected as a plant variety? The USA already provides the most liberal scenario, providing both patent and PVP option to protect plant and plant varieties. The European Union has also issued a Directive on the legal protection of biotechnological inventions to clarify how patent laws should be applied to biotechnological inventions. The genes used for transforming the transgenic varieties may be construed to be biotechnological inventions and considered eligible for patent by some countries. However, others may not consider gene as 'invention' but only 'discovery', which cannot be patented. Judgment would rely only on the respective national patent laws. From the discussion above it is proved that India provides as liberal protection by providing both patent and plant variety protection to seeds of Genetically Modified crops as given by the USA.

The most important thing to assess is the possible implications, on the various stakeholders, of the new IPR regime in India, which are enacted in an attempt to fulfill the obligations under WTO. There are many issues emerging in the area of agriculture with respect to agricultural biotechnology esp. G M crops, which may have grave significance over agriculture in future that need to be looked into in time.

For example Indian Protection of Plant Varieties and Farmers' Rights Act simultaneously protects the rights of breeders, farmers, researchers and public interest as well, whereas the new Patent Act makes way for product patent on seeds giving way to creating monopolistic rights. What are the possible implications of establishing such a system of multiple rights on the utilization and exchange of genetic resources among various actors? Could the attempt to distribute ownership rights to various stakeholders pose the threat of an 'anti-commons/ where resources are under utilized due to multiple ownership? Although the Multiple Rights system aims to equitably distribute rights, it could create problems of overlapping claims and result in complicated bargaining requirement for utilization of varieties. A potential implication is an 'anti-common tragedy' where too many parties independently possess the right to exclude giving rise to under utilization of resources. India and other developing nations, in seeking to achieve the important goal of recognizing the farmer's rights, must not overlook the need for promoting exchange of agricultural resources.

It is thus advised that the Indian government should, instead of fulfilling its obligation in haste, shall make such amendments in the act, which adequately safeguard and protect the interests of the domestic industries and market, taking advantage of the concessions given in the TRIPs agreement. Giant agribusiness MNCs today straddle the fields of biotechnology, fertilizers and pesticides, and patent monopolies would raise the possibility of their gaining control over our agriculture. So unlike what the government claims, the issue is not about sticking to a deadline to meet an international obligation, but about voluntarily signing away major sectors of our economy to Multinational Corporations. This is what the Indian parliament needs to really debate upon in the coming session.

REFERENCES

1. Bunn E; Turner S. R.; Panania M. and Dixon K. W., The contribution of *in-vitro* technology and cryogenic storage of conservation of indigenous plant. Aust. J. Bot., 55; 345-355., 2007.

2. Kapila .Raj, 'Indian Agriculture in the Changing Environment', 1st edition., Print Perfect Publications, New Delhi 2002.

3. Slidde, P. and Sonnino, A. Biotechnologies for the management of genetic resources for food and agriculture. Adv. Genet., 78;167 2012

4. Tysagi, Y.D., 'Modern Text Book on Botany', 1st edition., Universal Publications, Allahabad 1985.

5. Wadhera. B.I., 'Law Relating To Patents', 2nd edition., Universal Law Publication, New Delhi 2000.

Chapter-12

INTELLECTUAL PROPERTY RIGHTS AND ENTREPRENEURS

SARITA SHRIVASTAVA AND D B RAI SHRIVASTAVA*
Department of Zoology, *Department of mathematics,
S. M. S. Govt. Model Science College, Gwalior (MP)

It is well known globally that the patters of accumulation led growth have contributed powerfully to rapid and broad-based income generation, social progress and poverty reduction in India. But the same growth model of the past decades will not be adequate or sustainable in meeting the changing aspirations and multiplying needs of future generation, this is not just because of the inevitable decrease in social and economic returns to capital in the long term there are also absolute limits to the accumulation and utilization of tangible resources economic, social, demographic and environmental. The transformation could be needed through the entrepreneurship to bring about the productivity and growth by knowledge formation, ongoing innovation and life-long learning and competence building in India, but such a transformation can also be necessary with intellectual property right as a sequential progression in development, strategy and policy in India. Present paper is based on the IPR and entrepreneurs.

INTRODUCTION

Research & development and the accelerating progress in science and technology have been a backbone of the global information, resolution and development. The capital accumulation alone will not be adequate to sustain development under the economy and new global competition (N.V. Lam, 2005). People have ideas all the time in business , research and development. New idea can lead to new product and services and also generate value to the economy by encouraging people to invest in new development. Entrepreneurship is the occupation of excellence, charecterestic, practice and skill of a person stirring for the growth by creating innovation and organizing venture for enabling people to avail innovation to meet their need or solve people"s problems (Akhori 2013).Intellectual property is any product of human intellect that is intangible but has value in market place it is called IP because it is the product of human imagination, creativity and inventiveness (U. Kaiser, 2008). Intellectual property right are provided as a protection and incentive to creators, whose creativity could otherwise be freely used by others. Rights are granted for fixed period of time and protect only the fixation of creativity in material form (Shrivastava, 2013) IPR contributes enormously to our national and state economies. Dozen of industries across our economy relay on the adequate inforcement of their patent, trademarks and copyrights, while consumers use IP to ensure that they are purchasing safe guaranteed product (GIPC 2009).

ENTREPRENEUR

In political economics entrepreneurship is the quality of being an entrepreneur that is one who undertakes enterprise. An entrepreneur is someone that creates a new business. This can carry a high risk because it requires money to setup a new business without knowing if it will give a return on investment. Entrepreneurs need to have a good understanding of their market. Idea---Can this be turned into a marketable proposition --- protect the idea established IPR ---Setup on enterprise.

Dhirubhai Ambani was the greatest example of the sprit of entrepreneurship. In a short span of less than 25 years, and without even the benefit of a formal education. He built Reliance a first generation enterprise. He had just five hundred rupees in his pocket, a vision of what he wanted to achieve an intrinsic faith in latent demand potential of Indian market ,a belief in the capabilities of Indian people, and burning desire to succeed.

To set up a new business an entrepreneur needs to follow several steps
-Develop new products and services

For example an enterprise in Himachal Pradesh making Tofu from soya milk was launched about three years back. Tofu was a new product for the consumers, and made from completely nature ingredients due to high protein value it is beneficial for health. This new idea enabled to break into market that was dominated by existing products -Check that ideas are new. Entrepreneur need to carry out a search of registered intellectual property to check that their ideas does not already exist, and further information on IPR should search.

- Investigate if there are any barriers to setting up the business, will the business need to comply with any legal requirements.
- Raise finance for the business.

Means of Finance

All business need capital to operate-long term capital can be obtained from

- The owners on money and saving
- Their investors by offering shares in the new enterprise
- Banks, other institution in the form of loans and grants.

Business can raise substantial sums in this way. However, investors will want a share of profits and possibly some voice in running of the business. Bank will expect a business to pay interest or any loan. The entrepreneur may also have to offer some asset such as their own house, as security against the loan. The business will also need short term capital.

Business for entrepreneurs

All entrepreneurs must also decide what type of business to establish. There are three main type of small business. Each has distinct form and structure

Sole traders: A sole trader is a business owned by one person. Many plumbers, electrician, and other traders people work in this way. A sole trader may employ other people to assist on job to take phone calls or do the book keeping. It is simple to set up a sole trader business. There are some legal formalities -Sole trader have complete control of their business. They make their own decision and take all the profits for themselves, however sole trader can find it difficult to raise capital and they have liability for any debts incurred by the business this means that sole traders potentially risk even their savings, their homes and others assets of their business runs into trouble.

A Partnership: These involve two or more people working together. The partners share the workload and the profits of the business. Partners will have often have skills that complement each others and they can benefit from each others ideas. Partnership often find difficult to obtain capital. Most partnership do not have limited liability. This means that each partner can be held responsible for all debts incurred by the partnership

A company: This is a legal entity. It is owned by shareholders. The shareholders bring capital into the business. Shareholders take less risk than sole trader or partnership because they have legal protection called limited liability, this means that if the business cannot meet its debts then the maximum sum that shareholders can loss is limited to their investment in the company. Company decision making is steered by a board of directors.

Why do entrepreneur protect their ideas

Protection of idea for the creativity is essential because it can be copied and exploited by the others. For entrepreneur the idea is often the entire basis, the business would not exist. Entrepreneur invest money to develop business Benefits -IPR provides entrepreneur with many benefits

- IPR provides protection against a competitor directly copying the idea this helps the entrepreneur to recover their cost in developing the idea.

- IPR help business to maintain their long term competitive edge. Registered IP ensures that entrepreneur get all the financial benefits from their ideas.

- Registered IP is an asset. It helps to convince financial institutions to invest in a business enabling more money to be raised for development.

- Registered IP gives consumers confidence that products meet appropriate standards and quality.

- By being able to profit from their IP entrepreneur are rewarded for taking risk and developing new innovations. They can invest profit in work on new ideas.

- Ownership of the IP enables entrepreneur to licence or franchise ideas to others without risk. This means entrepreneur are able to expand the market for their product and services more easily and can increase revenue for the business.

How do entrepreneur protect their ideas

There are four categories of IPR. Each gives a different protection and is used for different purposes.

Patents-Patents are the inventions. Entrepreneur can seek patents for a new product or a new process that can be used in industries A patents can prevent others businesses from making, using, importing or selling similar products. To apply for patents a business must submit a patents specification. This is a written description, often with drawing of the invention. This sets out what the invention does and provides important technical details. A patent can last up to 20 years, if it is renewed every year.

Design-Registering a design prevents a competitor copying the physical appearance of a product includes line, shape, ,texture colours and materials. A registered design lasts initially for 5 years although it can be renewed for up to 25 years. for example registering designer fashions will stop others from using those designs This helps to protect design from being copied and appearing as cheap fakes on high street.

Trademarks-Trademarks is a sign that can distinguish goods and services from those of others traders. A sign can include a combination of words logos and pictures. To registered trademarks it must be

- Distinctive for a group of goods and services.

- Not the similar to any earlier marks on the register for the same goods and services. A trademark is a marketing tool which helps to develop and distinguish the brands. The trademark also provides reassurance for consumers. People will recognize product more easily when they see them advertised. Trademarks can last indefinitely provided that they are renewed every 10 years Entrepreneur register trademarks, design and logos to protect and represent their brand. Branding delivers huge commercial value to company. Many people recognize brands rather than individual product or services.

Copyright-It is an IPR that relates to the expression of an idea not the idea itself, for example any one can write a book or story based on research work but that can not copy the name, the text or illustration from other book about the same subjects Copyright protect the expression of an idea and not the idea it self. it protect photographs, original artistic, musical works. Copyright is an unrejected right, if applies as soon as something is created. There is no registration process or fee. it covers both printed and web based materials. IP also covers concept as trade secrets, plant varieties and performs right. Often more than one type of IP may apply to the same creations

Effect of IPR on entrepreneurs

Recent literature on the impact of IPR on developing countries have provided (Frink and Brega1999) foreign direct investment (Smarzynska2004) and economic growth (Thompson1999). Entrepreneur tends to spot changes swiftly. IPR protection provides a mechanism for entrepreneur to appropriate her or his returns to innovation, however the effectiveness of IPR protection of the extent to which the innovator can fully capture the returns varies according to the type of protection used and nature of innovation (Teece1986). Baumal (2002) state that the inherent characteristics of the entrepreneur , when the reward structure is an economy changes, either due to political, institutional or market reasons entrepreneur will be the first few economic agents who would identify the opportunities from the changes and respond to them. So it can be suggested that direct effect of IPR protection on the economy. According to Intan 2007 that strengthening of IPR protection in a green country would change the payoff structure of the economy by increasing potential return from undertaking the innovative activities.

CONCLUSION

The present century is century of knowledge. A nation ability to convert knowledge into wealth and social goods through the process of innovation is going to determine its future. Innovation was an integral part of ancient Indian civilization and culture. IPR refers to creation of mind i. e. inventions.IPR encourage innovation and reward entrepreneur. Risk and failure are the lifeblood of the innovation economy. IPR incentinize entrepreneur to keep pushing for new advances in the face of adversity. IPR facilitate the free flow of information by sharing the protection know how critical to the original, patented invention. In turn this leads to new innovation and improvement on existing one. Entrepreneurial manifestations and development are much wider phenomena, in any long run programme for developing or increasing entrepreneurial supply both in quality and number, many aspects of social and culture life will have to be included. It would mean inculcation such input of culture, education and training that the recipient becomes motivated and take to entrepreneurial pursuits. These could be brought under the purview of policy measures through several fundamental changes and over a long enough period. Only then can innovation and technological creativity take roots in a community and then almost become a habit for its members. In the wider perspective of economic development of underdevelopment countries, such an approach is very relevant.

REFERENCES

1. Akhouri M. M. 2013.,FDP on entrepreneurship M. I. T. S Gwalior.

2. Baumol W. 1993., Entrepreneurship management and structure of payoff. Camb., London Mit press.

3. Fink C. and C. A. P. Barga., 1999. How stronger protection of IPR affect international trade flows.

4. G. I. P. S. 2009 . Why are IPR important Global I. P. C.

5. Intan M. ,H. Livramento. 2007. Does IPR Protection affect growth of entrepreneur. Odyssea. CH, 1051, LAUSANNE.

6. Kaiser U. S. 2008. Importance of IPR Instit. for business economics , Zurich

7. Lam N. V. ,2005., A Perspective on entrepreneurship and IPR., Bulletin on asia pacific perspec.

8. Smarzynska Javorcik B., 2004. The composition of foreign investment and protection of IPR Europeon Economic review 48, 39, u 62.

9. Shrivastava S. and A. Shukla, 2013. National Seminar on IPRs, Morena (MP).

10. Teece d. j. 1986., Profiling from technological innovation implication for integration licencing and public policy., research policy 15, 285.

11. Thompson M. and F. Rushing. 1999. An empirical analysis of the impact of patent protection on economic growth . J. of Econo. Development. 24 (1). 67.

Chapter-13

INTELLECTUAL PROPERTY RIGHTS AND ITS IMPORTANCE

A. K. UPADHYAY, A. S GAHLAUT * AND N. K. BHARDWAJ

Department of Physics, Govt. P.G. College, Morena (MP).
* Department of Chemistry, Govt. P.G. College, Morena (MP).

The term intellectual property began to use in late 18th century. The use of term intellectual property was done by German confederation to grant legislative power for protection of intellectual property. In Paris and Berne convention also adopt the term intellectual property. In 1967, World Intellectual Property Organization (WIPO) is treated as agency of United Nations. The history of patents was initially granted by Queen Elizabeth I to provide monopoly privileges. After 200 years, a patent represents a right obtained by an inventor providing exclusive control over production and sale of his invention. According to French law, all new discoveries or inventions are the exclusive right of author to ensure the inventor the property for certain years. The purpose of intellectual property law is to encourage innovation for limited period. The common types of intellectual property rights consists patent, copyright, trademark and some trade secrets. Patent provides an exclusive right to make, use, sell to inventor for a limited period of time. While copyright gives the creator of an original work exclusive rights to it usually for a limited time. It does not cover ideas and information.

The objective of most intellectual property laws is to promote innovation. By providing limited exclusive rights for limited period, an incentive is created for inventor for their work. The World Intellectual Property Organization (WIPO) treaty related international agreements are promised that the protection of intellectual property rights is essential to maintain economic growth. Intellectual property is increasingly crucial to the economic, cultural and social well-being of every country. Intellectual property enriches our lives by providing us with work, entertainment and education. It is very different to think of a service, product or activity which in some way does not depend on intellectual property.

Industries dependent of intellectual property are central of our cultural life. No one can imagine life without film industry, music industry, publications, software and computer game, sporting events, fashion industry and globally recognizable brands. All these industries cannot survive without intellectual property laws. Prosperity of every country is dependent on intellectual property as the economy shifts its focus from assembly to products that require highly skilled employees, investment in research and development along with other key contributions to the economy. Protection of intellectual property protects investment in innovation.

Intellectual property can be known as property because it can be bought and sold, exchanged, traded, hired out. It has commercial character. Intellectual property is always attached to a physical thing but intellectual property itself is not a physical thing, upon which, or in which, it is carried. If you purchase a book or CD, you get the legal title to that particular object. But you do not own intellectual property right contained within the object. The right to claim authorship or to copy it is not yours. So purchase of book or CD is sharply different from purchase of copyright. If someone purchases the copyright, he also purchases the right of reproduce. The sale of copyright by inventor to anyone does not abolish the inventor's moral right. The inventor remains the inventor whether he sold the copyright. If any company sells the rights to distribute the information to any other company, they have paid the source of information for that information.

Thus intellectual property has three aspects:

- Moral right of inventor to protect the form of work and known as inventor.
- Business right of copyright holder to reproduce and distribute the work of inventor.
- Right of those who have paid for permission of use of work

As we discussed above that intellectual property exists in the form of patents, copyright and trademarks and industrial designs. There are different legal provisions for these forms. But copyright is the most common form of intellectual property. It is very hard to believe that copyright should be respected. Everyone has the right to the protection of the moral and material interests. Illegal copying or CDs and DVDs attracts such attain i.e. piracy. The material interests of copyright holders are being affected in terms of loss of revenue which belongs to copyright-holders. Although copyright did not affect ordinary public. Copyright regulated commercial relations between author, publisher and distributor.

In today's world, intellectual capital is considered to be a part of company's assets and it is constantly assessed, valued, and even listed in balance sheet. Intellectual property rights include one among many different categories given below. In some cases, a creation may be protected under more than one form of intellectual property rights. Patents are granted for invention that must have industrial applicability.

A patent, one granted in a particular jurisdiction, provides exclusively rights from the state for a fixed period of time in exchange for a full disclosure of the invention. Trademarks are the distinctive sign used to denote goods or products. It is done in order to establish uniqueness of a product supplied by one company from similar product of other companies. They are usually a combination of one or more words, letters, signs, symbols, drawing, colour and 3-D signs. Service marks are similar to trade marks, except they are use to designate services instead of products. Collective marks are the marks used to distinguish goods or service produced or provided by members of an association. Certification marks are used to distinguish goods or services that comply with a set of standards and have been certified by a authority. Copyright is a form of intellectual property protection available to all forms of expression of ideas, procedures, methods of operation etc. Copyrights are automatic rights, in that the protection is obtained by virtue of creation by the copyright owner. Trade secret is the information that is deliberately kept a secret from public for an economic benefit or a competitive edge for the owner. The main difference between trade secret and other form of intellectual property rights is that trade secret is the only one that is obtained by not disclosing the information to the public, whereas all other forms of protection is obtained by necessarily disclosing it.

In industry, product counterfeiting is a very big problem. Recently more attention is being paid to fighting the problem. The first step is to determine the size of counterfeiting market. It is very difficult task. No direct measurement of such trade can be undertaken. It is a problem back 2000 years. Counterfeiting of coinage was a normal exchange mainly in medieval India particularly in Tuglak dynasty. In France, supporters of Pope were minting counterfeiting coinage of real one issued by Protestant king. But product counterfeiting may even be older used by Babylonian and Egyptian priests. Some form of trademark has been in use since ancient time mainly in China's pottery and mudra used by business community in Sindhu civilization. Roman builders used the marker on bricks and titles to identify them. During middle ages, guilds affix marks on their products which distinguished from other.

Product counterfeiting came to attention of US government more than 100 years ago, when counterfeiting goods are export by UK mainly Manchester mills. Of course USA has not innocent of piracy. Estimates for the size of worldwide counterfeit goods market seem to be around 600 billion dollars annually. Now-a-days China is the main source of counterfeiting items. Anywhere that the international community attempts to establish good practice standards for industry, counterfeiters undercut them. Enforcement against intellectual property right violators was weak and penalties were inconsistently. India is generally defensive regarding intellectual property rights.

Moreover recently, the protection of intellectual property has become a matter of key importance in trade. Information digitalization and spread of computer network, copyright affects the entire population. But due to protection of intellectual property, public interest is also harmed. Integrated circuits have become integral component of our daily life. They form part of every appliance we use in our daily life. The key feature of an IC is the presence of multiple circuits on a thin substrate of semi-conductor. Design of ICs is protected under intellectual property right. USA was the first to introduce a suitable system for protection of semi-conductor ICs layout design in 1984, and several countries follow the same path. But the basics of physics such as Newton's laws of motion and Einstein mass-energy relation are all ideas that cannot be protected. All such law belongs to nature and is for everyone. Copyright laws do not allow for the protection of mathematical formulae. For example "Energy is equal to multiplication of mass with square of speed of light" cannot be copyrighted because it is the common way to explain energy. Publication of papers in journals and conferences are all copyright material but fundamental theories cannot be copyright. Scientific data are copyright but method used to obtain data cannot be copyright. Similarly Software programs are protected under copyright but idea behind o develop software cannot be protected under copyright. In India, copyright held sixty years after last the life of author. While it is valid for sixty years for the date of release under cinematography and book's publication.

REFERENCES

1. Anderson, Birgitte, " Intellectual property rights : Innovation, Governance and Institutional".

2. Gupta,TamaliSen, "Intellectual property laws in India".

3. Talwar, Sabanna, Intellectual property rights and Human Development in India".

Chapter-14

BIOINFORMATICS AND IP ISSUES: AN OVERVIEW

SADHNA PANDEY

Department of Botany, Govt. K.R.G. P.G. College, Gwalior (M.P.)

The fundamental unit of life is a cell contains DNA that comprises genes, encoding RNA which in turn produces proteins. These proteins regulate all of the biological processes within an organism. Thus life can be visualize as information technology. Information coded in DNA flows from it to RNA and then to protein which expressed in a trait.

The human body is made up of an estimated millions of cells each of which possess 23 pairs of chromosomes that are comprised of 30,000 genes made up of 3 billion pairs of DNA bases. A large number of genome projects are being carried out world-wide in order to identify all the genes and their function in specified organisms. With the completion of human genome project in 2000 and development of high throughput techniques, a large amount of data is generated through genome sequencing protein profiling etc. And here the role of information technology in biological sciences became indispensible. Since then the bioinformatics has gone a sea change.

Broadly bioinformatics describes any use of computers to handle biological information. The National center for Biotechnology information (NCBI) 2001 defines bioinformatics as "Bioinformatics is the field of Science in which biology , computer science and information technology merge into a single discipline".

Bioinformatics is conceptualizing biology in terms of molecules (in sense of physical chemistry) and applying informatics techniques (derived from discipline such as applied mathematics, comp. science and statistics) to understand and organize the information associated with these molecules, on a large scale. In short bioinformatics is management information system for molecular biology and has many practical applications.

There are three important sub disciplines within bioinformatics:

(i)   Organization of biological data

(ii) Development of tools and resources that are used in analysis of data

(iii) Application of tools in analysis and interpreting the result in biologically meaningful manner.

Major Bioinformatics Events

Some of the major events in rise and growth of bioinformatics are:

1930 – Introduction of Electrophoresis technique by Tiseleus for separating proteins in solution.

1951 - Pauling and Corey propose the structure for the alpha- helix and beta sheet for protein

1952 – Alfred Day Hershey and Martha Chas proved that DNA carriers genetic information

1953 – Watson and Crick proposed double helix model of DNA

1965 – Margaret Dayhoff's Atlas of protein sequence

1970 - Needleman Wunsch alogorithm for sequence comparisons

1972 – The first rDNA molecule created by Paul Beg

1973 – The Brook Haven protein data bank is announced

1975 – E M Southern published the experimental details for Southern Blot technique and specific DNA sequence

1977 - Full description of Brookhaven PDB was published

1977 – Allan Maxam , Walter Gilbert and Frederick Sanger presented method for sequencing DNA

1981 – Smith Waterman alogorithm

1981 – Concept of sequence motif (Doolittle)

1982 – Phage lambda genome sequenced

1983 – Sequence data base searching algorithm (Wilbeer-Lipman algorithm)

1985 – FASTP/FASTN : Fast sequence similarity searching

1985 – Kary mullis described Polymerase chain reaction

1986 – The word "genomics" coined by Rodericks

1986 – Creation of SWISS-PROT database by Deptt. of Medical Bichem at Univ. of Geneva and European Molecular Biology Laboratory

1987 – Computer language – Perl related by Larry Wall

1988 – Human genome project initiated

1988 – National Center for Biotechnology information (NCBI) was created at NIH/ NLM.

1988 – EMBnet work for database distribution

1990 – BLAST Fast sequence similarly search

1991- Creation and use of expressed sequence Tags(ETS) was described by Craig Venter et. al.

1992 – The institute for genomic research established by Craig Venter

1994 – The PRINTS database of protein motifs is published by Attwood and Beck

1995 – The Heamophils influenza genome 1.8(Mb) sequenced

1996 – Baker's yeast (12.1) Mb was sequenced

1997 – Genome of E. coli. (4.7 Mbp) was published

1998 – Celera was formed by Craig Venter

2000 – Genome of Pseudomonas aeruginosa and Arabidopsis thaliana genome published

2001 – The human genome published

2004 – Rat genome project published

With the unprecedented growth in software developments and invention of new techniques in biological sciences bioinformatics finds its roots in all spheres of biological science applications.

Sequence Analysis

Major biological molecules are classified as nucleic acids (DNA and RNA) Proteins, lipids and carbohydrates. Bioinformatics currently focuses on biological information contained in DNA, RNA and protein. In bioinformatics complete genome analysis includes (a) genome sequence analysis (b) gene finding/ gene annotation and sequence comparison.

Genome sequencing includes managing, processing and analyzing the DNA sequences. Shot gun sequencing is one of the most common method used for genome sequencing. Process involves shearing of DNA and then pieces of DNA are assembled , cloned and sequenced. Many softwares are available for this purpose including Phred/Phred/consed(http://www.phrap.org).Arachne(http://www. broad.niit.edu/wg), GaP4(http://staden.sourceforge.net/overview/html), AMOS(http://www.tigr.org/software/AMOS) (a modular open source package develop by TIGR). Some other recently developed methods for sequence analysis including differential hybridization of olegonucliotide probs, polymorphism rate sequences, Four colour DNA sequencing by synthesis on a chip and 454 method based on micro fabricated high density picoliter reactor.

Gene Finding and Gene Annotation

This involves primary analysis of genome for identification of protein coding genes i.e. prediction of introns and exons in a segment of DNA sequence. A number of computer program, software are available for identifying for this purpose.

gen.scan(http://genes.mitedu/GENSSCAN.html)

genemark HMM(http://opal.biology.gatech.edu/genemark)

grail(http://copmbio.ornlgov/grail 1-3/)

genie – (http://www.frecilfly.org/seg-data/genic)

glemmer(http://www.tigr.org/softlab/glimmer)

Sequence Comparison

Sequence comparision is very important aspect of bioinformatics. It provides information about structure , function and evolution of gene and genome. Sequence comparison is based on similarity between two strings of text and may not provide accurate information about homology especially when the confidence level is low.

Different methods are used for sequence comparison – pair wise, sequence profile and profile-profile comparison. For pair wise sequence FASTA(http://fastabioch virginia.edu) and BLAST tools are most popular tools available.

For sequence profile alignment PSI-BLAST (http:// ncbi.nim.gov/BLAST) is popularly used tool. Some more accurate(but slower) software for sequence profile comparison are available.

HMMER(http://hmmer.wustl.edu)

SAM(http://www.cse.usc.edu/research/comparison)

Sam.html (longer protein) more 100.

META- MEME(http://metamem.sdsc.edu)

For sequence based comparison of proteins

Pfam(http://pfamwus+1.edu,proDOM(http://proteintoulose.Infra.fr/prodom/current/html/home.php)

For small conserved protein, commonly used tools arePROSIT(http:// aer.expasy.org.prosite/PRINTS),(http://unber.sbs.man.ac.uk. Dbbrowser/PRINTS) and BLOCKS(http://www.psc.edu general/software/package) blocks.html.

TRANSCRIPTOME

Transcriptome is the set of all RNA including mRNA, rRNA and other non-coding RNA produced in one or population of cells. Whole transcriptome analysis helps in understanding how altered expression of genetic variant contributes to complex disease development like Cancer, Diabetes and Heart diseases.

DNA microarray is widely used powerful technology applied for transcriptome analysis. Two general types of microarray are high density. Oligonucliotide array that contain a large number of (thousands sometimes billions) of relatively short probes synthesized directly on surface of arrays or arrays with amplified polymerase chain reaction products or cloned DNA fragments mechanically supported directly on the array surface. Common tools and software that perform variety analysis on large microarray data are gene traffic, genespreng(http://www.agilent.com/chemg exnspring),CaARRAY(http://caarray.nci.nih.gov/),Besides DNA microarray, whole genome array method and tilling array is also used for transcriptome analysis.

Software used for these methods include chip viewer (http://signalsalk.edu.cgiben/atta) and Integrated genome brower(IGB). Recently developed next generation in sequencing techniques are more efficient and give better results. A new software CPTR(Across-platform transcriptome analysis (http://people.tamee.edu/system, cpra/cpra.html) is powerful tool used for transcriptome profile analysis which can be used to analyze transcriptome profiling data from separate methods.

PROTEOMICS

Proteomics is component of bioinformatics dealing with qualitative and quantitative characterization of protein and their interactions on genome scale. It deals with identification and quantification of all proteins types in a cell or tissue analysis of post- harvest translational modifications and association with other proteins. Electrophoresis is most common method used for separation of proteins. Many bioinformatics tools have been developed for two-dimensional (2D) electrophoresis analysis SWISS-2DPAGE (http://an expasy org/melanin), Flicker (http:open2dropt sourceforge.net.flicker, PDQUEST http://www.proteomework.bio-red.com) is a another popular commercial software pachage for comparing 2D gel image. For identification of proteins mass spectroscopy is used . Protein identificationis also done by peptide finger printing and Tandem mass spectrometry(MS/MS) MOWSE(the latest version Emwose) is software for protein identification by PME.

MS/MS provide still better identification on amino acids in the peptide many software tools have been developed for MS/MS SEQUEST(http://fields.srips.edu/sequel) and mascot(http://www/maheisceence.com/).

METABOLOMICS

Metabolomics is the analysis of the complete pool of small metabolites present in a cell. In a given time. It aims to compare the relative difference between biological samples based on their metabolic profiles. It can provide instantaneous picture of entire physiology of an organism. It is metabolomics great importance in understanding, identifying secondary metabolites in plants. In metabolite profiling experiments metabolites are extracted from tissues separated and analyzed using high throughput technique. Various aspects of metabolomics can be studied using software E-cell(http:wwac.cell.org or cellDesigner, http://www system-biology.org).

Databases

Database is usually considered as compilation work. A database might not constitute potential subject matter as it is only preservation of information not a composition of matter that involves any modification or innovation. One of the most popular methods of protecting databases is through the copyright law. Copyright is the most efficacious form of protection conferred to databases. Copyright protects both databases producers and owners of the data that database producers may wish to use. The main drawback with copyright protection is that the content of the database may be copied and rearranged without the permission of inventor to design a new database of identical contents. For this purpose some countries have introduced a new "sui generis" law. Sui generis is a unique system of protection that protects the interest of maker as well as inventor. It becomes very useful especially in those countries which have not established effective protection laws. On databases with this law makers of databases prevent other parties from copying or accessing contents from database. Two forms of contract laws are available – shrenk wrap license and click wrap license. Shrink wrap license is used for databases in CDS and click wrap license is on the other hand used for internet databases. The term of contract generally includes restriction on use of databases, prohibit a third party from accessing the content or forbid down loading or transmit data.

BIOINFORMATICS AND IP ISSUES

Biology has always been information driven science. Computers play an important role to store, retrieve analyze and predict the composition, structure and function of biomolecules. As the new high throughput (next generation sequence) technologies evolved, so was the growth of information technology and evolution of computers. Thus bioinformatics is an interdisciplinary science – an interface between biological and computational sciences. In recent times researchers are working to make sense of wealth of data that has been stored and analyzed. Bioinformatics finds its place in fields of agriculture, healthcare and medicine, environment conservation etc. It has added a new dimension to drug designing and personal medicines. With this interest a copious amount of funding is pouring into research and development of bioinformatics tools by govt. agencies, pharmaceutical companies and software companies. It is with interest researchers in the field of bioinformatics seek some form of legal protection for their innovations in terms of bioinformatics tools like other innovations. Intellectual property protection is the key factor for economic growth and technical advancements in the society. These intellectual property protection add value to tab new discoveries /innovations. Intellectual property laws are driving forces for the innovation.

The law of intellectual property comprises following distinct categories.

Patent Act: Whoever invent or discover any new and useful process machine, manufacture (apparatus) or composition of matter or any new and improvement there may obtain a patent therefore.

The patentee thus has-

(i) Exclusive right to prevent their particular from using patented article.

(ii) sell whole or a part of his patent

(iii) Can also grant license to other to use their patents property.

(iv) Can also assign such property to any other patentable invention must have
(i) novelty(ii) inventive steps and industrial applications.

The grant of patent confers the exclusive right of use on the patentee for commercial gain but the act also recognizes that govt. may use any invention over even without the payment to inventor. The idea of patent can be put to use for general public, benefit and the patentee would have to forgo his commercial gain in the general public interest.

Copyright Protection

Copyright protection subsist an original work of authorship fixed in any tangible medium of expression. It is available for works of authorship such as literary music etc. Copyright protection does not cited to any idea, procedure, process system, method of operation, concept, principle or discovery.

Trade Secret

Information including – a compilation, program device method that derives independent economic value, actual or potential from not being generally known to and not being readily ascertainable by proper means by other person who can obtain economic value from its disclosure or use and the subject of effort that are reasonable under the circumstance to maintain its secrecy.

Scope of TP protection for bioinformatics can be split into major components: biological sequences tools in and bioinformatics software /hardware in retrieval and analysis of data.

Biological Databases

Databases that are available via Web and internet have now become indispensible tool for biological research. Three types of databases have been established – (i) large scale public repositories (ii) community specific databases and (iii) project specific databases. Large scale public repositories are usually developed and maintained by government agencies or international consortia. These are the places where long term data are stored ex. Gene bank for sequences, uniport for protein information, Protein data bank for protein structure and information. Array express and gene expression omnibus(GEO) for microarray data.

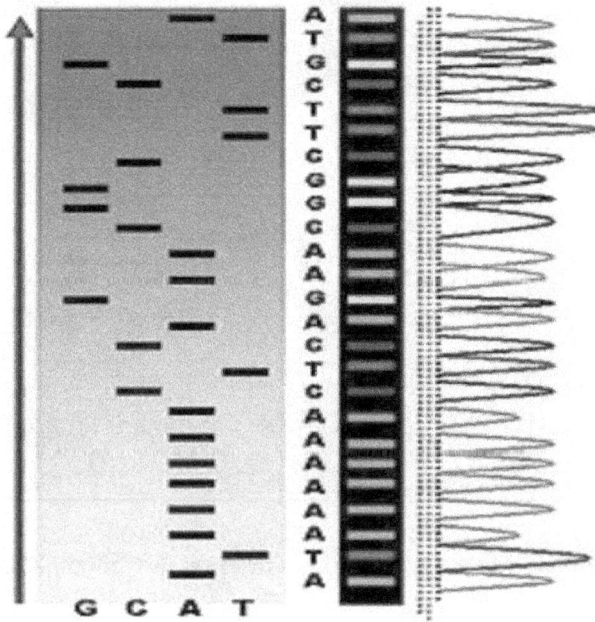

Fig- 01, Radioactive_Fluorescent_Seq.

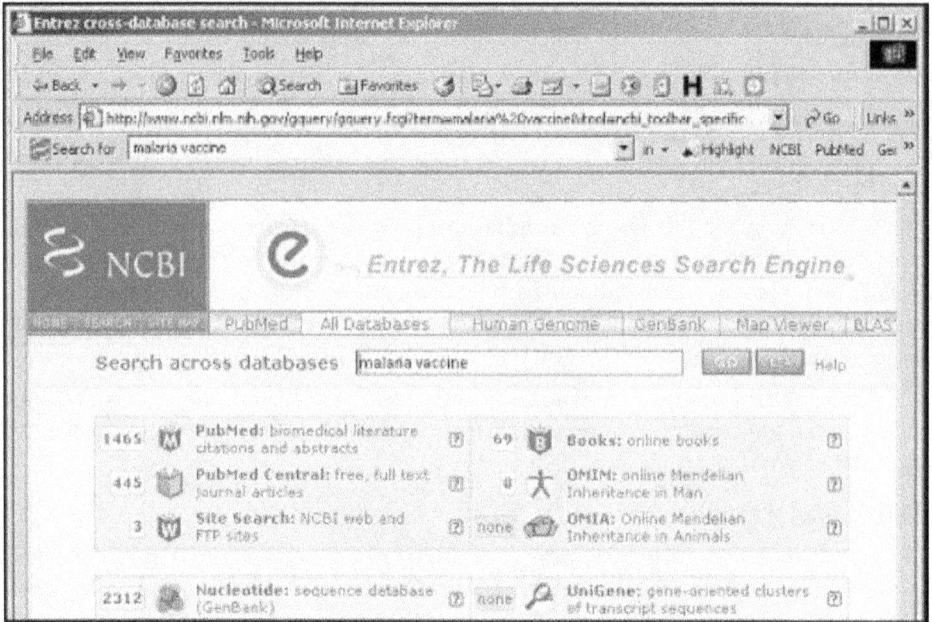

Fig -02, Toolbar

Fig-03 Automated-DNA-Sequencers-For-Human-Genome-Project

Community specific databases typically contain information eurated with high standards and support the need of a particular community of researchers. Ex. Clade oriented comparative databases on metabolism. The concept of community specific data bases subject to change as the scope of research widens.

The third category of databases are smaller scale databases and short lined that specifically developed for project data management, Often these databases and web resources are not maintained beyond the completion of project.

Biological Sequences

Biological sequences are not patentable since it may not be characterized as natural phenomenon. Copyright protection is also not available for biological sequences because they are not copy rechargeable subject matter because the scientist is not the original author of biological sequence, although he is the first person to report the sequence of novel molecule/genes. Moreover the sequence is only "discovery" which is not installed for copy right protection.

Bioinformatic software and hardware

Unlike biological sequences and databases, Bioinformatic software are eligible for patent protection. Bioinformatic software has biological applications which are useful, concrete and tangible. These software are used to make medical diagnosis, design drugs or draw evolutionary conclusions. Similarly Bioinformatic hardware are also eligible for patent protection as it comes under machine or an apparatus. In India there is no patent available for computer program coupled with some hardware components may fall under the scope of patentable subject matter. In India copy right protection is accorded to computer program (software) and defined to both source code and object code. Bioinformatic software can also be protected through the laws of trade secrets. Generally owners/ writers maintain the source as tread secrets releasing only the object code for sale of license. However there is a risk that tread secret may be disclosed by revere engineering. The danger of reverse engineering is also applied to customized bioinformatics apparatus which might be stopped down and each individual component analysis to disclose the protected trade secrets.

REFERENCES

1.   http:/wiki bioinformatics.org-of-bioinformatics (26 Aug. 2007).

2.   Jagadish A T (2013). Int.Journal Scientific and Research Publication Vol. 3

3.   Scott M and M C Bude. Bioinformatics and intellectual property protection, Berkeley Technology Journal, (2002), 7:1.

4.   Aebersold R, Mann M (2003). Mass spectrometry-based proteomics, Nature 422:198-207.

5.   Alfarano C, Andrade CE, Anthony K, Bahroos N, Bajee M et. al (2005). The Biomolecular Interaction Network Database and related tools 2005 update, Nucleic Acids Res., 33: D418-24.

6.   Bino R, Hall R, Fiehn O, Kopka J, saito K et. al (2004). Potential of metabolomics as a functional genomics tool, Trends Plant Sci., 9:418-25.

7.   Blake J (2004). Bio-ontologies-fast and furious, Nat. biotechnol., 22:773-74.

8.   Blueggel M, Chamrad D, Meyer HE(2004). Bioinformatics in proteomics, Curr. Pharm. Biotechnol, 5:79-88.

9.   Brown P, Botstein D (1999). Exploring the new world of the genome with DNA microarrays,Nat. Genet., 21:33-37.

10.   Gras R, Muller M (2001). Computational aspects of protein identification by mass spectrometry, curr. Opin. Mol. Ther. 3:526-32.

Chapter-15

WTO, TRIPS AND INDIAN AGRICULTURE

V. S. MTSANIYA AND PAWAN AHIRWAR
Department of Economics,
Dr. Hari Singh Gaur Central University, Sagar (MP)

For around 75 per cent of the world's population, the mainstay of livelihood is agriculture, particularly in the developing countries. And yet both qualitative and quantitative improvements in this sector have been marginal almost in all the countries during the last several decades. India ranks 2nd in farm output among all the countries of the world and around 60 per cent of India's population depend on this sector for rural employment. Agriculture accounted for 14.6 per cent of India's GDP and 10.6 per cent of country's exports in the first half of 2009-2010.

Current agricultural practices in India are neither economically viable nor environmentally sustainable; the reasons being overregulation of agriculture, small holdings, lack of irrigation and dependency on nature (monsoon), technological gaps. Government policies, agricultural subsidies, credit problems etc.

WORLD TRADE ORGANIZATION (WTO)

After several rounds of negotiations, the Uruguay round led to the signing of GATT agreement at Marrakesh in Monaco in April 1994, one of the key elements being the establishment of the WTO in January 1995 in Geneva. The WTO's scope extended beyond matters of merchandise trade, to agriculture, textiles and clothing, investments, innovation, competition policies, safeguard measures, trade in services, anti-dumping, sanitary and phyto-sanitary measures e4tc. All the member states, currently numbering 153, have tacitly agreed to all the provisions of the new world order subject to their national legislations endorsing the provisions within the overall ambit of WTO's mandate.

Outside the UN, the WTO is the largest single body to develop and implement a world trade order which will benefit all members through universally accepted rules. As such, it is imperative that it succeeds. From the WTO perspective, one of the major issues confronting the members in 2009 was the closing of a fresh round of negotiations to finalize the Doha Development Round. If the stalemate largely prompted by protectionist tendencies by the members continues, it is uncertain whether the Doha Development Round will be finalized even in 2011.

The establishment and functioning of WTO and all its attendant departments were expected to improve international trade by uniformly applying harmonized systems in global trade, for both the developed and developing countries in equitable measures. There have already been concerns whether these objectives are likely to be realized even in the mid to long term. This concern is particularly relevant to two vital areas, namely, health and food security. To what extent such concerns are justified in the light of several legislations in different countries on matters related to a uniform intellectual property rights protection system as defined under TRIPS is a question, which begs a satisfactory answer.

TRADE RELATED INTELLECTUAL PROPERTY RIGHTS (TRIPS)

The most important component of GATT as far as knowledge and innovation based industrial segments are concerned is the TRIPS Agreement. It was already recognized during the trade negotiations that countries of the world not only differ widely in their economic and developmental status but also in their capability to develop or even utilize modern technology. That was the reason for providing transitional periods (Article 65) in the TRIPS Agreement whereby developing countries had up to a ten year period (2005) and the least developed countries 21 till 2016 (original 16 years extended to 21 at the Doha summit in 2001) for implementation. Thus while the time frame for implementation was different for different countries based on their socio-economic background and development as far as the terms and provisions are concerned, their socio-economic background and development as far as the terms and provisions are concerned there is only one homogenous and uniform standard. Considering the inequities inherent in applying the same standards across all members regardless of their developmental needs, special provisions for developing countries were brought in, particularly those with healthcare needs including access to drugs. Even though the Doha Declaration was expected to bring in a paradigm shift in overcoming issues related to affordability and accessibility of patented drugs through compulsory licenses, in reality its practice has been made very complex by the TRIPS Council and consequently has remained effective. However, an equally important issue is the impact of TRIPS council and consequently has remained effective. However, an equally important issue is the impact of TRIPS on food security through removal of restrictions imposed by TRIPS on patented agricultural products including germplasm plant varieties seeds, processed foods etc. This issue was not addressed at Doha because matters related to agriculture are dealt with under the AOA and is one of the key elements of discussion in the Doha Development Agenda.

PROTECTION OF BIOTECHNOLOGY INVENTIONS

One of the most controversial issues in recent times has been the evolution and emergence of genetically modified organisms (GMOs), in the agriculture and food segments. The desirability of patenting life forms and genetic engineering based processes and products, has by itself been questioned. TRIPS makes it mandatory to provide protection of microorganisms (without defining the term), one of the essential components of biotechnology based inventions. Such processes have the potential to improve productivity of food products apart from the ability to produce more specific and better quality foods. The best known example of a patented technology and product is Monsanto's golden rice which produces beta carotene helpful in the alleviation of blindness. Apart from the health benefits that such foods provide, the technology has the potential to improve the productivity in the agricultural sector. However, in the wake of wide spread criticism about GM crops, there has been a considerable slowdown in R&D and commercialization activities in this area.

SANITARY AND PHYTO-SANITARY (SPS) MEASURES

Matters related to food safety and the impact of release of genetically modified materials on the environment could fall under yet another safeguard instrument, the SPS measures stipulated as a major trade issue by WTO. These measures were meant to minimize the negative effects of poor quality drugs and foods circulating in international trade and restricting access to them in national markets. SPS measures should be nondiscriminatory, follow international standards, ensure transparency and have fair inspection procedures.

GEOGRAPHICAL INDICATIONS ACT

In principle, the TRIPS Agreement mandates a minimum standard for protection of Geographical Indications (GIs) under Article 22.2 to be used in cases where there was prima facie evidence of malpractice including misleading the customer to the geographical origin of the product. However the Agreement specifically men tions under Article 23, that GIs related to wines and spirities have to be protected whether or not they mislead the customer. This distinction or in fact discrimination has been pointed out by many members, after the Agreement came in force, as being discretionary and needs amendments.

CLIMATE CHANGE AND AGRICULTURE

The very first legal framework to provide for balancing the need for conservation and sustainable utilization of plant genetic resources as well as a procedure for ABS was initiated by the FAO in 2001 under the International Treaty on Plant Genetic resources for Food and Agriculture (ITPGRFA). Prior to this. A UN inter-governmental forum to deal with matters related to the conservation and utilization of genetic resources for food and agriculture under the Commission on Genetic Resources for Food and Agriculture (CGRFA) was set up, which also monitored the implementation of International Undertaking on Plant Genetic Resources (IUPGR), 1983. The IUPGR was the first non-legally binding agreement to deal with international matters related to plant genetic resources. In 1997, CGRFA established working groups on plant genetic resources covering technical and policy issues that facilitated the intergovernmental negotiations for the revision of IUPGR in harmony with the provisions of the Convention on Biological Diversity (CBD).

PROTECTION OF TRADITIONAL KNOWLEDGE IN AGRICULTURE

Most of the agricultural practices, particularly in developing countries stem from indigenous and traditional knowledge systems seldom documented. They are extremely valuable for the sustenance of those practices and ensuring food security for large populations. The IP protection systems currently in vogue and stipulated under the TRIPS agreement are unsuitable for protecting such traditional knowledge and practices. Realizing the importance of such knowledge and the need to protect them to afford economic advantage to those in possession of such knowledge assets, several international agencies including world Intellectual Property Organization (WIPO), WHO, Food and Agricultural Organization (FAO); various national governments and national and international non-governmental organizations have been working on developing a fair and equitable system to protect traditional knowledge, indigenous medicinal plants, food crops etc., which will be acceptable to all members of WTO and the global community. A special sui generis form of legislation which will meet the requirements is being proposed by WIPO, some of the members of WTO and others, but nothing of substance has emerged so far.

TRADE SECRETS

TRIPS provides for protection of trade secrets of undisclosed information under Article 39. Trade secrets are protected for unlimited time. However, to qualify for protection, it is to be ensured that information to be protected is actually a secret, has indeed commercial value and every effort has been made to maintain its secrecy. Theoretically, if a farmer wants to keep the undisclosed technology or process used by him his operations secret,it can be protected under this provision,but in actual practice it is hard to implement these provisions since most, if not all, activities in the agricultural sector are in the public domain with a multitude of stake holders, practitioners and participants.

CONCLUSION

Developing countries have a log at stake to ensure that agriculture their mainstay for survival and growth are given their rightful place in the international for a dealing with global agreements productions costs and market access in the field of agriculture. The WTO responsible for bringing a new world trade order benefiting all the stake holders consists of a number of multilateral agreements most of which have a bearing on agriculture. There have been very little efforts to consolidate these agreements analyse their relative contributions and develop strategies which shall result in economic gains to countries whose primary livelihood rests on agriculture. While there are enough provisions to ensure that equity is assured when dealing with issues related to agriculture based on the plethora of international agreements what is needed is their proper interpretation and effective implementation.

REFERENCES

1.   http://www.wto.org/english/tratop_e/trips_e/t_agmo_e.htm (1December 2010).

2.   http://www.wto.org/english/tratop_e/sps_e.htm (1December 2010).

3.   http://www.ebd.int/ (1 December 2010).

4.   Nair M D. How far has the Doha Round gone? Journal of Intellectual Property Rights, 14 (6) (2009) 542-543.

5.   Reddy A and Chatterjee S, A critique of the Indian law and approach towards protection of GI, Journal of Intellectual Property Rights, 12 (6) (2007) 572-580.

6.   Mittal R and singh G, Patenting activities in agriculture from India, Journal of Intellectual Property Rights, 10 (4) (2005) 315-320.

7.   Kowalski S, Rational risk/benefit analysis of genetically modified crops, Journal of Intellectual Property Rights, 12 (1) (2007) 92-103.

8.   Harshawardhan and Keshri S, Trade secrets: A secret to unveil, Journal of Intellectual Property Rights, 13 (3) 2008 208-2017.

9.   Report of the Inter Governmental Committee on Intellectual Property, Genetic resources. Traditional Knowledge and Folklore, 16th Session, Geneva, 3-7 May 2010.

Chapter-16

INTELLECTUAL PROPERTY RIGHTS & THEIR IMPORTANCE IN BIOTECHNOLOGY

MAMTA GUPTA

Department of Botany, M.J.S. Govt. P.G. College, Bhind-477001, MP (India)

IPR is a general term covering patents, copyright, trademarks, industrial designs, geographical indications protection of layout design of integrated circuits and protection of on disclosed information. These rights gives statutory expression to the moral and the economic rights of creators in their creations. IPR are rights granted to creators and owners of works that are the results of human intellectual creativity. Basically IPRs are essential for the incentive to create easily copied products. These works can be in the industrial, scientific, literacy or artistic domains. They can be in the form of an invention, a manuscript, a suite of software, or a business.

INTRODUCTION

Intellectual property is a product of the mind. Intellectual property (land) or physical property, which one can see, feel and use with any type of property there are property rights, when IPS are expressed in a tangible form, they can also be protected. Intellectual property rights have been created to product the right of individuals to enjoy their creations and discoveries.

The convention establishing the Wondate intellectual property organization in 1967. Once of the specialized agencies of the United Nations system, provided that "Intellectual property" shall include rights relating to -

(1) Literacy, artistic, scientific works;

(2) Performance of performing artistics, phonograms and broad casts;

(3) Inventions in all fields of human endeavour;

(4) Scientific discoveries;

(5) Industrial designs;

(6) Trademarks, service marks, and commercial names and designations; and

(7) Protection against unfair completion and all other rights resulting from intellectual activity in the industrial.

Intellectual property is protected and governed by appropriates national legislation. The national legislation specifically describes the inventions that are the subject matter of protection and those which are excluded from protection. For example, method of treatment of the humans or animals by surgery or therapy, inventions whose use would be contrary to law or morality or inventions which are injurious to public health are excluded from patentability in the Indian legislation.

TYPES/TOOLS OF IPRs.

(a)   Patents

(b)   Trademarks

(c)   Copyrights and related rights

(d)   Geographical Indications.

(e)   Industrial Designs.

(f)   Trade Secrets.

(g)   Layout Design for Integrated Circuit.

(h)   Protection of New Plant variety.

(a) Patient: A patent is a government granted exclusive right to an inventor to prevent others from practicing i.e. making, using or selling the invention. A patent is a personal property that can be licensed or sold like any other property. It provides protection for the invention to the owner of the patent. The protection is grathed for a limited period, i.e. 20 years. Patent protection means that the invention can not be commercially made, used distributed or sold without the patent owner's consent. A patent owner has the right to decide who may or may not use the patented invention for the period in which the invention is protected. The patent owner may give permission to, or license, other parties to use the invention on mutually agreed term. The owner may also sell the right to the invention to someone else, who will then become the new owner of the patent. Once a patent expires, the protection ends, and an invention enters the public domain, that is, the owner no. Longer holds exclusive rights to the invention, which becomes available to commercial exploitation by others.

Most biotechnology inventions are filed as utility patents and not as plant patents. As a utility patent, it is possible to protect plant genes rather than just the plant, and to control the use of genetic material of a number of plants and for multiple uses such as disease resistance herbicide resistance, or pharmaceutical or oil production (Chawla, 2002).

(b) Trademarks: A trademark is a distinctive sign that identifies certain goods or services as those produced or provided by a Specific person or enterprise. It may be one or a combination of words, letters, and numerals. They may consist of drawings, symbols, Three - dimensional signs such as the shape and packaging of goods, audible signs such s music or vocal sounds fragrances, or colours used as distinguishing features. It provides protection to the owner of the mark by ensuring the exclusive right to use it to identify goods or services, or to authorize another to use it in return for payment.

It helps consumers identify and purchase a product or service, because its nature and quality, indicated by its unique trademark, meets their needs.

Trademark rights are so important that multinational companies spend large amount of money to maintain this respective trademarks around the word. Every country has different trademark laws, However, there are agreements to ensure that a company's trademark in one country is protected in another country. India has a Trade and merchandise Act enacted in 1958 that has been amended in 1999.

In biotechnology research laboratory equipments bear trademarks that are well known to workers in their field. Certain vectors useful in recombined - DNA technology are also known by their trademarks.

(c) **Copyrights and related rights:** Copy right is a legal term describing rights given to creators for their literacy and artistic works. The kinds of works covered by copyright include : Literacy works such as novels, poems, Plays, reference works, newspapers and Computer programs; databases; films, musical compositions, and choreography; artistic works such as painting, drawing photographs and sculpture; architecture; and advertisements, Maps and technical drawings. Copyright subsists in a work by virtue of creation; hence it's not mandatory to register. However, registering a copyright provides evidence that copyright subsists in the work & creator is the owner of the work (Nichols Bentley, 1999).

In biotechnology, the copyright may cover DNA sequence data that may be published. However, an alternative sequence coding for some protein may be prepared using wobble in the genetic Code, So that the copyright is not infringed.

(d) **Geographical Indications:** Geographical Indications are signs used on goods that have a specific geographical origin and posses qualities or a reputation that are due to that place of origin. Agricultural products typically have qualities that desire from their place of production and are influenced by specific local factors, such as climate and soil. They may also highlight specific qualities of a product which are duc to human factors that can be found in the place of origin of the products, such as specific manufacturing skills and traditions.

A geographical indication points to a specific place or region of production that determiner the characteristic qualities of the product that originates there in. It is important that the product derives its qualities and reputation from the place. Place of origin may be a village or town, a region or a country.

(e) **Industrial Designs:** Industrial designs refer to creative activity, which result in the ornamental or formal appearance of a product, and design right refers to a novel or original design that is accorded to the proprietor of a validly registered design. Industrial design is on element of intellectual property. (David Kirkpatrick, 2002).

The essential purpose of design law it to promote and protect the design element of Industrial production. It is also intended to promote innovative activity in the field of industries.

(f) Trade Secrets : It may be confidential business information that provides on enterprise a completive edge may be considered a trade secrets. Usually these are manufacturing or industrial secrets and commercial secrets. These include sales methods, distribution methods, consumer profiles, advertising strategies, lists of suppliers and clients and manufacturing processes. Contrary to patents, trade secrets are protected without registration.

A trade secret can be protected for an unlimited period of time but a substantial element of secrecy must exist, so that, except by the use of improper means, there would be difficulty in acquiring the information. Considering the vast availability of traditional knowledge in the country the protection under this will be very crucial in reaping benefits from such type of knowledge. The Trades secret, traditional knowledge are also interlinked / associated with the geographical indications. (Singh, 2004).

(g) Layout Design for Integrated circuits: Semiconductor Integrated circuit means a product having transistors and other circuitry elements, which are inseparably formed on a semiconductor material or an insulating material or inside the semiconductor material and designed to perform an electronic circuitry function.

The aim of the semiconductor Integrated circuits Layout - Design Act 2000 is to provide protection of Intellectual property Right (IPR) in the area of semiconductor Integrated circuit Layout Designs and for matters of the seed industry.

The plant variety protection and formers Rights act 2001 was enacted in India to protect the new plant variety; the act has come into force on 30.10.2005 through Authority.

Initially 12 Crop species 12 Crop species have been identified for regt. i.e., Rice, Wheat, Maize, Sorghum Pearl, Millet, Chickpea, Green gram, Black gram, Lentil, Kidney bean etc. India has opted for sui-generic system instead of patents for protection new plant variety. Department Agriculture and Cooperation is the administrative ministry looking after its registration and other matters. (Digital Dilemma, 2000)

CONCLUSION

Intellectual property right has a great importance in research, business and industry also without intellectual property right we can not protect any business, research and industry for example when a intents and invention then be has no worry of theft by some one about it his invention. The same conditions is in business and industry also, so in conclusion we can say that without intellectual property right we can not protect any research, business and industry and biotechnology.

REFERENCES

1.   Chawla, H.S. (2002). Introduction to Plant Biotechnology (Second edition).

2.   David, Kirkpatrick (2002). Tuning out the customer fortune com. Tuesday, October, 8.

3. The Digital Dilemma (2000). Intellectual property in the Information Age, CSIB Executive Summary.

4. Nichols, Bentley (1999). Intellectual; property in the information Age Computer Science and Telecommunication Board (CSTB).

5. Sing, B.D. (2004). Biotechnology; First edition reprinted 2008, Kalyani Publication, Ludhiana.

Chapter-17

INTELLECTUAL PROPERTY RIGHTS: A REVIEW

PRATIBHA YADAV[a], RENU SINGH[b], DINESH K. CHATURVEDI[c] & AMIT K. S. CHAUHAN[d]

[a]Holkar Science College,Indore (MP), [b]Govt. Girls College, Bhind (MP)
[c]MJS Govt. PG College, Bhind (MP), [d]Govt. PG College, Morena (MP)

Intellectual property rights are like any other property right. They allow creators, or owners, of patents, trademarks or copyrighted works to benefit from their own work or investment in a creation. These rights are outlined in Article 27 of the Universal Declaration of Human Rights, which provides for the right to benefit from the protection of moral and material interests resulting from authorship of scientific, literary or artistic productions.

The importance of intellectual property was first recognized in the Paris Convention for the Protection of Industrial Property (1883) and the Berne Convention for the Protection of Literary and Artistic Works (1886). Both treaties are administered by the World Intellectual Property Organization (WIPO).

HISTORY

The World Intellectual Property Organization (WIPO) is one of the specialized agencies of the United Nations (UN) system of organizations. The "Convention Establishing the World Intellectual Property Organization" was signed at Stockholm in 1967 and entered into force in 1970. However, the origins of WIPO go back to 1883 and 1886, with the adoption of the Paris Convention and the Berne Convention respectively. Both of these conventions provided for the establishment of international secretariats, and both were placed under the supervision of the Swiss Federal Government. The few officials who were needed to carry out the administration of the two conventions were located in Berne, Switzerland.

Initially there were two secretariats (one for industrial property, one for copyright) for the administration of the two conventions, but in 1893 the two secretariats united.

The most recent name of the organization, before it became WIPO, was BIRPI, the acronym of the French-language version of the name: United International Bureaux for the Protection of Intellectual Property (in English). In 1960, BIRPI moved from Berne to Geneva.

At the 1967 diplomatic conference in Stockholm, when WIPO was established, the administrative and final clauses of all the then existing multilateral treaties administered by BIRPI were revised. They had to be revised because member States wished to assume the position of full governing body of the organization (WIPO), thus removing the supervisory authority of the Swiss Government, to give WIPO the same status as all the other comparable intergovernmental organizations and to pave the way for it to become a specialized agency of the United Nations system of organizations.

Most of the intergovernmental organizations now called specialized agencies did not exist before the Second World War. They were created for the specific purpose of dealing with a particular subject or field of activity at the international level. However, some intergovernmental organizations, such as the International Labour Office (ILO), the Universal Postal Union (UPU) and the International Telecommunication Union (ITU) were in existence, and had become the responsible intergovernmental organizations in their respective fields of activity long before the establishment of the United Nations. After the United Nations was established, these organizations became specialized agencies of the United Nations system.

Similarly, long before the United Nations was established, BIRPI was the responsible intergovernmental organization in the field of intellectual property. WIPO, the successor to BIRPI, became a specialized agency of the United Nations when an agreement was signed to that end between the United Nations and WIPO which came into effect on December 17, 1974.

A specialized agency, although it belongs to the family of United Nations organizations, retains its independence. Each specialized agency has its own membership. All member States of the United Nations are entitled to become members of all the specialized agencies, but in fact not all member States of the United Nations are members of all the specialized agencies. Each State decides for itself whether it wants, or does not want, to become a member of any particular specialized agency. Each specialized agency has its own constitution, its own governing bodies, its own elected executive head, its own income, its own budget, its own staff, its own programmes and activities. Machinery exists for coordinating the activities of all the specialized agencies, among themselves and with the United Nations, but basically each agency remains responsible, under its own constitution, to its own governing bodies, which are the States members of the organization.

The agreement between the United Nations and WIPO recognizes that WIPO is, subject to the competence of the United Nations and its organs, responsible for taking appropriate action in accordance with its basic instrument and the treaties and agreements administered by it, inter alia, for promoting creative intellectual activity and for facilitating the transfer of technology related to industrial property to developing countries in order to accelerate economic, social and cultural development.

TYPES OF IPRs

a. Patents.

b. Trademarks.

c. Copyrights and related rights.

d. Geographical Indications.

e. Industrial Designs.

f. Trade Secrets.

g. Layout Design for Integrated Circuits.

h. Protection of New Plant Variety.

a. Patent

A patent is an exclusive right granted for an invention, which is a product or a process that provides a new way of doing something, or offers a new technical solution to a problem. It provides protection for the invention to the owner of the patent. The protection is granted for a limited period, *i.e* 20 years. Patent protection means that the invention cannot be commercially made, used, distributed or sold without the patent owner's consent. A patent owner has the right to decide who may - or may not - use the patented invention for the period in which the invention is protected. The patent owner may give permission to, or license, other parties to use the invention on mutually agreed terms. The owner may also sell the right to the invention to someone else, who will then become the new owner of the patent. Once a patent expires, the protection ends, and an invention enters the public domain, that is, the owner no longer holds exclusive rights to the invention, which becomes available to commercial exploitation by others.

All patent owners are obliged, in return for patent protection, to publicly disclose information on their invention in order to enrich the total body of technical knowledge in the world. Such an ever-increasing body of public knowledge promotes further creativity and innovation in others. In this way, patents provide not only protection for the owner but valuable information and inspiration for future generations of researchers and inventors. General Principles governing the Patent System in India and further details can be viewed at DIP&P website at http://ipindia.nic.in/ipr/patent/patents.htm

b. Trademarks

A trademark is a distinctive sign that identifies certain goods or services as those produced or provided by a specific person or enterprise. It may be one or a combination of words, letters, and numerals. They may consist of drawings, symbols, three-dimensional signs such as the shape and packaging of goods, audible signs such as music or vocal sounds, fragrances, or colours used as distinguishing features. It provides protection to the owner of the mark by ensuring the exclusive right to use it to identify goods or services, or to authorize another to use it in return for payment. It helps consumers identify and purchase a product or service because its nature and quality, indicated by its unique trademark, meets their needs. Registration of trademark is prima facie proof of its ownership giving statutory right to the proprietor. Trademark rights may be held in perpetuity. The initial term of registration is for 10 years; thereafter it may be renewed from time to time. General Principles governing the Trademarks System in India and further details can be viewed at DIP&P website at http://ipindia.nic.in/tmr_new/default.htm

c. Copyrights and related rights

Copyright is a legal term describing rights given to creators for their literary and artistic works. The kinds of works covered by copyright include: literary works such as novels, poems, plays, reference works, newspapers and computer programs; databases; films, musical compositions, and choreography; artistic works such as paintings, drawings, photographs and sculpture; architecture; and advertisements, maps and technical drawings. Copyright subsists in a work by virtue of creation; hence it's not mandatory to register. However, registering a copyright provides evidence that copyright subsists in the work & creator is the owner of the work.

Creators often sell the rights to their works to individuals or companies best able to market the works in return for payment. These payments are often made dependent on the actual use of the work, and are then referred to as royalties. These economic rights have a time limit, (other than photographs) is for life of author plus sixty years after creator's death. General Principles governing the Copyrights and related rights System in India and further details can be viewed at website of Copyright Office website at http://copyright.gov.in/

d. Geographical Indications (GI)

GI are signs used on goods that have a specific geographical origin and possess qualities or a reputation that are due to that place of origin. Agricultural products typically have qualities that derive from their place of production and are influenced by specific local factors, such as climate and soil. They may also highlight specific qualities of a product, which are due to human factors that can be found in the place of origin of the products, such as specific manufacturing skills and traditions. A geographical indication points to a specific place or region of production that determines the characteristic qualities of the product that originates therein. It is important that the product derives its qualities and reputation from that place. Place of origin may be a village or town, a region or a country. It is an exclusive right given to a particular community hence the benefits of its registration are shared by the all members of the community. Recently the GIs of goods like Chanderi Sarees, Kullu Shawls, Wet Grinders etc have been registered.

Keeping in view the large diversity of traditional products spread all over the country, the registration under GI will be very important in future growth of the tribes / communities / skilled artisans associated in developing such products. General Principles governing the Geographical Indication System in India and further details can be viewed at website of Geographical Indication Registry, website at http:// ipindia.nic.in/girindia.

e. Industrial Designs

Industrial designs refer to creative activity, which result in the ornamental or formal appearance of a product, and design right refers to a novel or original design that is accorded to the proprietor of a validly registered design. Industrial designs are an element of intellectual property. Under the TRIPS Agreement, minimum standards of protection of industrial designs have been provided for. As a developing country, India has already amended its national legislation to provide for these minimal standards. The essential purpose of design law it to promote and protect the design element of industrial production. It is also intended to promote innovative activity in the field of industries. The existing legislation on industrial designs in India is contained in the New Designs Act, 2000 and this Act will serve its purpose well in the rapid changes in technology and international developments. India has also achieved a mature status in the field of industrial designs and in view of globalization of the economy, the present legislation is aligned with the changed technical and commercial scenario and made to conform to international trends in design administration. This replacement Act is also aimed to enact a more detailed classification of design to conform to the international system and to take care of the proliferation of design related activities in various fields. General Principles governing the Industrial Design System in India and further details can be viewed at DIP&P website link at http://ipindia.nic.in/ipr/design/designs.htm.

f. Trade Secrets

It may be confidential business information that provides an enterprise a competitive edge may be considered a trade secret. Usually these are manufacturing or industrial secrets and commercial secrets. These include sales methods, distribution methods, consumer profiles, advertising strategies, lists of suppliers and clients, and manufacturing processes. Contrary to patents, trade secrets are protected without registration. A trade secret can be protected for an unlimited period of time but a substantial element of secrecy must exist, so that, except by the use of improper means, there would be difficulty in acquiring the information. Considering the vast availability of traditional knowledge in the country the protection under this will be very crucial in reaping benefits from such type of knowledge. The Trades secret, traditional knowledge are also interlinked / associated with the geographical indications.

g. Layout Design for Integrated Circuits

Semiconductor Integrated Circuit means a product having transistors and other circuitry elements, which are inseparably formed on a semiconductor material or an insulating material or inside the semiconductor material and designed to perform an electronic circuitry function. The aim of the Semiconductor Integrated Circuits Layout-Design Act 2000 is to provide protection of Intellectual Property Right (IPR) in the area of Semiconductor Integrated Circuit Layout Designs and for matters connected there with or incidental thereto. The main focus of SICLD Act is to provide for routes and mechanism for protection of IPR in Chip Layout Designs created and matters related to it. The SICLD Act empowers the registered proprietor of the layout-design an inherent right to use the layout-design, commercially exploit it and obtain relief in respect of any infringement. The initial term of registration is for 10 years; thereafter it may be renewed from time to time. Department of Information Technology Ministry of Communications and Information Technology is the administrative ministry looking after its registration and other matters. General Principles governing the Layout Design for Integrated Circuits System in India and further details can be viewed at DIT website link at http://mit.gov.in/default.aspx?id=322

h. Protection of New Plant Variety

The objective of this act is to recognize the role of farmers as cultivators and conservers and the contribution of traditional, rural and tribal communities to the country's agro biodiversity by rewarding them for their contribution and to stimulate investment for R & D for the development new plant varieties to facilitate the growth of the seed industry. The Plant Variety Protection and Farmers Rights act 2001 was enacted in India to protect the New Plant Variety; the act has come into force on 30.10.2005 through Authority. Initially 12 crop species have been identified for regt. i.e. Rice, Wheat, Maize, Sorghum, Pearl millet, Chickpea, Green gram, Black gram, Lentil, Kidney bean etc. India has opted for sui- generic system instead of patents for

protecting new plant variety. Department Agriculture and Cooperation is the administrative ministry looking after its registration and other matters. General Principles governing the Protection of New Plant Variety System in India and further details can be viewed at Protection of Plant Varieties and Farmers' Rights Authority, India (PPV&FR) website link at http://www.plantauthority.gov.in.

The objective of the scheme is to enhance awareness of MSME about Intellectual Property Rights (IPRs) to take measure for the protecting their ideas and business strategies. Effective utilisation of IPR tools by MSMEs would also assist them in technology upgradation and enhancing competitiveness. These initiatives are proposed to be developed through Public-Private Partnership (PPP) mode to encourage economically sustainable models for overall development of MSMEs. Underthis programme financial assistance will be provided for taking up the identified initiatives. Eligible applicants/beneficiaries will have to contribute minimum 10% of the GoI financial support for availing assistance under the scheme. The detail guidelines, eligibility criteria, funding pattern and prescribed format etc. are available on http://www.dcmsme.gov.in/schemes/Guidelines-UK.pdf

CONCLUSION

We see, then, that a system of property rights in "ideal objects" necessarily requires violation of other individual property rights, e.g., to use one's own tangible property as one sees fit. Such a system requires a new homesteading rule which subverts the first occupier rule. IP, at least in the form of patent and copyright, cannot be justified. It is not surprising that IP attorneys, artists, and inventors often seem to take for granted the legitimacy of IP. However, those more concerned with liberty, truth, and the institutionalized use of force used to enforce IP rights. Instead, we should re-assert the primacy of individual rights over our bodies and homesteaded scarce resources. rights should not take for granted.

REFERENCES

1. http://ipindia.nic.in/tmr_new/default.htm
2. http://copyright.gov.in/
3. http://ipindia.nic.in/tmr_new/default.htm
4. http://ipindia.nic.in/ipr/design/designs.htm
5. http://mit.gov.in/default.aspx?id=322
6. http://www.plantauthority.gov.in.
7. http://mit.gov.in/default.aspx?id=322
8. http://www.dcmsme.gov.in/schemes/Guidelines-UK.pdf

Chapter-18

HOW TO GET A PATENT IN INDIAN SYSTEM

KESHAV S. JATAV[1], R. P. SINGH[2], BRAJESH K. JATAV[3] & MADHUP SHRIVASTAV[4]

[1]*Department of Botany, Govt. Chhatrasal College Pichhore, Shivpuri (MP)*
[2]*Department of Botany, Govt. P G College Morena (MP)*
[3]*Department of Botany, Govt. P G College Datia (MP)*
[4]*School of Studies in Botany, Jiwaji University, Gwalior (MP)*

The term 'Patent' has been defined under the patent act 1970 as an exclusive right granted by government to the owner of invention to use, manufacture and market the invention for a limited period of time. The new invention may be a new and useful process, machine, composition of matter, or any new and useful improvement thereof. The patent act prohibits others from making, using or selling the invention. However the use of a patent may be affected by other laws of the country which has awarded the patent. A patent in the law is a property right and hence, can be gifted, inherited, assigned, sold or licensed. The patent right is territorial in nature and inventors/ their assignee will have to file separate patent applications in countries of their interest, along with necessary fees, for obtaining patents in those countries. After the expiry of the period for which exclusive right is granted to the inventor, the invention can be put to use by any person other than the one to whom a patent had been granted.

THE INDIAN PATENT ACT

The first Indian patent laws were first promulgated in 1856. New patent laws were made after the independence in the form of Indian Patent Act 1970 and were modified time to time. The most recent amendment was made in 2005 which were preceded by the amendments in 2002 and 2003. The act has now been radically amended to become fully compliant with the provisions of TRIPS. The Indian patent act 1970 and the patent rules, 1972 regulate the grant, the operative period, the revocation and infringement, etc., of the patents.

India is the member of the following international organization and treaties:

1. WIPO Convention, since May 1975.
2. Paris Convention (Industrial Property), since December 1998.
3. Berne Convention (Literary and Artistic Works), since April 1928.
4. PCT (Patents), since December 1998.
5. Geneva Convention (Unauthorized Duplication of Phonograms), since February 1975.
6. Budapest Treaty (Deposit of Micro-organisms), from December 2001.
7. Nairobi Treaty (Olympic Symbol), since October 1983.
8. WTO: Member and Signatory to TRIPS Agreement, since January 1995.
9. UCC since October 1957.
10. SAARC since December 1985.

Definition of an invention

An invention can be defined as a new product or process involving an inventive step and capable of industrial application. New invention means any invention or technology which has not been published in any document or used in country or elsewhere before the date of filling patent application with complete specifications.

What can be patented?

All the inventions, processes and product are patentable which posses:

(1) **Newness/Novelty:** means it should not be published in India or elsewhere, in prior public knowledge or prior public use within India or elsewhere in the world. Basically, if an invention is not new, it is not patentable.

(2) **Inventiveness/ Non- obvious:** means a feature that makes a invention not obvious to a person of ordinary skill in the art and a technological advancement to the existing art or inventive steps.

(3) **Usefulness:** The invention besides new, non- obvious must also be useful or capable of being used in an industry.

What cannot be patented?

Some inventions in spite of being new, non-obvious and useful cannot be patented under the act are:

(1) Inventions which are injurious to public health or violet public morality or public interest.

(2) New method of agriculture or horticulture is non patentable invention in order to have a more widespread benefit of such invention rather than concentrating the commercial gain of such invention in the hands of inventor alone.

(3) A process of treatment of human beings, animals or plants cannot be patented.

ESSENTIAL PATENT DOCUMENTS TO BE SUBMITTED

There are two types of patent documents usually known as patent specification, namely-

(1) **Provisional Specification:** A provisional specification is usually filed to established priority of the invention in case disclosed invention is at conceptual stage and a delay is expected in submitting full and specific description of the invention.

(2) **Complete Specification:** It very essential to submit complete specification to obtain a patent. The contents of a complete specification would include:

(a) Title sufficiently indicating the subject matter to which the invention belongs.

(b) A full and particular description of invention along with experimental results.

(c) Background of the invention including prior art giving drawbacks of the known invention practices.

(d) Drawing etc. essential for understand the invention.

(e) Claims related to a single invention or to a group of invention should be clear and succinct.

(f) A declaration as to inventor ship of the invention.

PROCEDURE FOR OBTAINING A PATENT

Where to apply?

Section 6 to 11 of the act lists the conditions to the applicant while submitting application for grant of a patent. Patent Application can be filed by an inventor, alone or jointly with others, or his/their assignee or legal representative of any deceased inventor or his assignee. Application for the patent has to be filed in the respective patent office as mentioned below. The territorial jurisdiction decides whether applicant falls in their territory or not on the basis of residence, place of origin of invention etc.

VARIOUS PATENT OFFICES IN INDIA

Patent Office	Territorial Jurisdiction
Delhi	States of Haryana, Himachal Pradesh, Jammu and Kashmir, Punjab, Rajasthan, UP, Uttaranchal, National capital territory of Delhi and union territory of Chandigarh.
Mumbai	States of Madhya Pradesh, Chhattisgarh, Maharashtra, Gujarat, Goa, union territory of Daman and Diu and Dadra and Nagar Haveli.
Chennai	States of Andhra Pradesh, Kerala, Karnataka, Tamilnadu and union territory of Pondicherry and Lakshadweep.
Kolkata (Head Office)	Rest of India

How to apply

Application for patent cab be obtained by payment of fee Rs. 1000 for natural citizen of India and 4000 for other than citizen. Following steps are involved in obtaining a patent:

(1) Application (Form 1) for patent should be file with either a provisional specification or a complete specification (Form 2). Only one application can be made for one invention.

(2) Submission of complete application, if provisional application was submitted earlier.

(3) Examination of application by patent office.

(4) Acceptance of applications and publication in the gazette of accepted applications.

(5) Acceptance of oppositions/objections if any and responding and satisfactorily overcoming them to grant of patent.

(6) Grant and sealing of patent.

TERM OF PATENT

Section 53 of the Act lays down the term of Patent after the commencement of the Patent Act, 2002 or the terms of every patent which has not expired and has not ceased to have effect, on the date of such commencement under this Act, shall be twenty years from the date of filling of the application for the patent.

COMPULSORY LICENCE

The term of patent can, however, be cut short by the grant of 'compulsory license' or 'license of right' to any person to work the invention when the patentee fails to work the invention in public interest.

REFERENCES

1. Anonymous (2007). A manual on intellectual property rights. Entrepreneurship Development and IPR unit, Birla Institute of Technology and Science, Pilani.

2. Anonymous (2008) Report of task force ministry of commerce and industry, December 12, 2008.

3. Patent and trade mark guide in India. India Juris Advocates & Corporate Legal Consultants Trade Mark & Patent Attorneys Delhi, India.

4. Kalyan C. Kankanala, Arun K. Narasani& Vinita Radhakrishnan, 'Indian Patent Law and Practice', 2010, Oxford University Press.

5. Intellectual property rights under WTO: Tasks before India / T Ramappa. - New Delhi: Wheeler Publishing, 2000.

Chapter-19

INTELLECTUAL PROPERTY RIGHT PROTECTION IN INDIA: A PERSPECTIVE

PRERNA MITRA, R P SINGH*, S S NIGAM** and D K SHARMA***

Department of Botany, Govt. P G College, Mandsaur (MP)*
Department of Botany, Govt. P G College, Morena (MP)
**Department of Chemistry, Govt. P G College, Morena (MP)
***Department of Zoology, S M S Govt. Model Science College, Gwalior (MP)

Property has been legally described as the right of a person or a group of persons that can be possessed by him. Anything is capable of being owned has to be taken as property. It means that all the creation of mind and skill of a person is the property of the creator. After the rapid evolution of science & technology and development of technology to have access over them through the great leaps in information technology is how to protect this property and provide the advantage to the genuine owner.

In India, protection of intellectual Property Right gained interest of people in about the middle of the last century. India thus enacted Indian Patent Act, 1970 to provide protection to the vast natural recourses, great heritages and traditions of the country. After that there are number of act draws its power and force from a variety of legislatures of the country since 1865 to 2000. Some important acts are as:

♦ Indian Penal Code, 1865.

♦ Code of Civil Procedure, 1908.

♦ Copyright Act, 1957.

♦ Specific Relief Act, 1963.

♦ Indian Patent Act (1970), amended in 1999 2002 and 2004 superseded by Patents Amendment Act 2005

♦ Trade Related Intellectual Property Rights Agreement (TRIPs) in 1995, as part of the treaty obligations, India was compelled to modify the Indian Patent Act (1970).

- Code of Criminal Procedure, 1973.
- Trade Marks Act, 1999.
- Geographic Indicators of Goods (Registration and Protection) Act, 1999.
- Industrial Designs Act, 2000.
- Information Technology Act, 2000.
- Protection of Plant Variety and Farmers' Rights (PPVFR) Act, 2001.
- Biological Diversity Act, 2002

THE SALIENT FEATURES OF THE PATENTS ACT, 1970

- Elaborate definition of invention
- No product patents for substances intended for use as food, drugs and medicines including the product of chemical processes
- Codification of certain inventions as non-patentable
- Mandatory furnishing of information regarding foreign application
- Adoption of absolute novelty criteria in case of publication
- Expansion of the grounds for opposition to the grant of a patent
- Exemption of certain categories of prior publication, prior communication and prior use from anticipation
- Provisions for secrecy of inventions relevant for defence purposes
- Provision for use of inventions for the purpose of Government or for research or instruction to pupils
- Reduction in the term of patents relating to process in respect of substances capable of being used as food or as medicine or drugs
- Enlargement of the grounds for revocation of a patent
- Provision for non-working as ground for compulsory licences of right, and revocation of patents
- Additional powers to Central Government to use an invention for purposes of government including Government undertakings
- Prevention of abuse of patent rights by making restrictive conditions in licence agreements/contract as void
- Provision for appeal to High Court on certain decisions of the Controller
- Provision for opening of branches of the Patent Office.

This Act remained in force for about 24 years till December 1994 without any change. An ordinance effecting certain changes in the Act was issued on 31th December 1994, which ceased to operate after six months. Subsequently, another ordinance was issued in 1999. This ordinance was later replaced by the Patents (Amendment) Act, 1999 that was brought into force retrospectively from 1st January, 1995. The amended Act provided for filing of applications for product patents in the

areas of drugs, pharmaceuticals and agro chemicals though such patents were not allowed. However, such applications were to be examined only after 31st December, 2004. Meanwhile, the applicants could be allowed Exclusive Marketing Rights (EMRs) to sell or distribute these products in India, subject to fulfilment of certain conditions.
1.2.11 The second amendment to the 1970 Act was made through the Patents (Amendment) Act, 2002 (Act 38 0f 2002). This Act came into force on 20th May, 2003 with the introduction of the new Patents Rules, 2003 by replacing the earlier Patents Rules, 1972. Salient features of the

PATENTS (AMENDMENT) ACT, 2002

- ♦ Further codification of non patentable inventions
- ♦ 20 years term of patent for all technology
- ♦ Provision for reversal of burden of proof in case of process patents
- ♦ Provisions of compulsory licences to meet public health concerns
- ♦ Deletion of provision of licence of right
- ♦ Introduction of system of deferred examination
- ♦ Mandatory publication of applications after 18 months from the date of filing
- ♦ Provision for process patent for micro organisms
- ♦ Establishment of Appellate Board
- ♦ Provision for parallel imports
- ♦ Provision for exemption from infringement proceedings for use of a patented invention for obtaining regulatory approval for a product based on that patented invention
- ♦ Provision to protect biodiversity and traditional knowledge.

The third amendment to the Patents Act, 1970 was introduced through the Patents (Amendment) Ordinance, 2004 w.e.f. 1st January, 2005. This Ordinance was later replaced by the Patents (Amendment) Act, 2005 (Act 15 of 2005) on 4th April, 2005 which was brought into force from 1st January, 2005.

THE SALIENT FEATURES OF THIS AMENDMENT

- ♦ Extension of product patents to all fields of technology including food, drugs, chemicals and micro organisms
- ♦ Deletion of the provisions relating to Exclusive Marketing Rights (EMRs)
- ♦ Introduction of a provision for enabling grant of compulsory licence for export of medicines to countries which have insufficient or no manufacturing capacity to meet emergent public health situations
- ♦ Modification in the provisions relating to opposition procedures with a view to streamlining the system by having both pre-grant and postgrant opposition in the Patent Office
- ♦ Strengthening the provisions relating to national security to guard against patenting abroad of dual use technologies

♦   Rationalisation of provisions relating to time-lines with a view to introducing flexibility and reducing the processing time for patent application.

PATENTS RULES

Section 159 of the Patents Act, 1970 empowers the Central Government to make rules for implementing the Act and regulating patent administration. Accordingly, the Patents Rules, 1972 were notified and brought into force w.e.f. 20th April, 1972. These Rules were amended from time to time till 20th May, 2003 when new Patents Rules, 2003 were brought into force by replacing the 1972 rules. These Rules were further amended by the Patents (Amendment) Rules, 2005 and the Patents (Amendment) Rules, 2006. The last amendments were made effective from 5th May, 2006.

Property rights with respect to patents, industrial designs, geographical indicator goods, softwares, IT etc. increase with the competent provisions of law. The monopoly of the same lies in favour of registration holder for a certain period.

The provisions of common law of trots are involved to redress the grievances and promise the establishment of the legal property right. The infringement of unregistered trade marks and copyrights is assured to occur when the reputation of original holder is misappropriated or goodwill is damaged.

IPR registration is not essential for trademark and copyright which covers-artistic work, literary work, audio records, video records, software, etc. On the other hand specific registration is necessary for patents, industrial designs, geographical indications, formulation etc.

IPRs can be cancelled on the basis of following points.

1.   Against any right of other person

2.   Against universal laws

3.   Misrepresentation

4.   Against any right of other person

5.   Mistakenly

6.   Against public policy or morals

The violation of IPR has to be tested through critical examination.

♦   Phonetic similarity

♦   Ocular similarity

♦   Likely hood of confusion and deception

♦   Microscopic comparison may show similarities

♦   Actual damage and/or loss not necessary

The legal remedies for the violation of IPR can either be civil or criminal. The civil remedies may lead to following:

♦ Accord of injunction /stay

♦ It may decide the clam of damage

♦ It can look into accounts and can order the person to handover the profit.

Interim order can be passed by the civil court. The order may grant injection either export or after hearing both the parties. The procedure to be adopted before the civil court shall involve.

1. Filing the case along with all the supporting documents indicating the infringement of IPR.

2. Filing of application under order 39 rules 1 and 2 read with section 151 of code of civil procedure for issuing an ex-parte stay order.

3. Filing application under section 26 of code of civil procedure for appointment of local commissioner.

4. Hearing the agreement and being satisfied the court may pass an order according ex-parte stay.

The jurisdiction for civil case shall involve:

♦ Where the cause of action has accrued

♦ Where the part of action has accrued

♦ Where the violation of law is taking place

♦ Where the defendants reside or work or gain

Competent courts for civil action shall be district and session judge of pecuniary and territorial jurisdiction. The court fee payable varies from state to state. Certain high courts *e.g.* Delhi High court have been authorized to entertain these cases directly.

Criminal remedies can be invoked by filing a criminal complaint before chief judicial Magistrate/Chief Metropolitan Magistrate of the concerned jurisdiction. The court after examining the evidences and application preferred u/s 91/93 of the code of criminal procedures shall issue an order for seizure/warrant. Alternately the court direct to police to investigate the case and lodge F.I.R. u/s/156 of code of criminal procedures.

The criminal action can be invoked u/s 103/104 of trade marks act, 1999, section 63 and 64 of copyright Act, 1957; section 39 of Geographic indicators of goods (registration and protection) Act, 1999; section 420 of Indian panel code 1865: section 91/93 of code of criminal procedures 1973 etc.

CONCLUSION:

It is concluded that India has enough legislative provisions to meet the exigencies and accord protection to Intellectual Property Rights. However, there is need of awareness among Research scholars, Teachers, Businessmen and common people.

REFERENCES

1. Anonymous (2008). Manual OF PATENT PRACTICE AND PROCEDURE THE PATENT OFFICE, INDIA

2. Das R R (2008). INTELLECTUAL PROPERTY RIGHT PROTECTION IN INDIA, Proceeding: National Seminar on Current Status and importance of IPR issues, JIwaji University, Gwalior, p.21-25

3. Kalyan C. Kankanala, Arun K. Narasani& Vinita Radhakrishnan, 'Indian Patent Law and Practice', 2010. Oxford University Press.

Chapter-20

INTELLECTUAL PROPERTY RIGHTS AND BIOSENSORS

VINAYAK SINGH TOMAR¹, N.S.DADORIYA², J.K. MISHRA & R.L. SAKHAWAR³

¹*Department of Zoology, Govt. P.G. College, Morena (MP)*
²*Department of Environmental Science, Govt. P.G. College, Morena (MP)*
³*Department of Botany, Govt. P.G. College, Morena (MP)*

The intellectual property is generally understood as a "product of the mind". It is similar to the property consisting of movable or immovable things like a house or a scooter, where in the owner may you his property as he wishes and nobody else can lawfully use his property without his permission. IPR is conferred in respect of works that result from the creative and inventive activities of the human mind. Main elements of IPR include the patents, copyright and relative rights, trademarks, geographical indications, industrial designs, layout designs and protection of undisclosed information. The rights are the legal rights, granted by the government, for a limited period, in exchange of the public discloser of the inventions. The grant of rights is intended to encourage the creators in their creative fields. The rights are governed according to the national and international laws.

INTRODUCTION

Biosensors are devices, usually miniature in size, providing real time, online monitoring of some biological materials. The biological materials have lead to technological interventions that modify the very building blocks of life forms. Many plants, animals, bacteria and fungi include useful biological materials within their cells the biological materials may be the whole of the micro-organisms as viruses, bacteria spores, plasmids, algae, fungi, vector gens etc. biosensor find application in medical diagnostics, analysis of food samples and in environmental monitoring. The aim of this paper is to study innovative activity in the field of biosensors.

METHODOLOGY

Information on patents can be searched by name of an inventor, name of the inventor is clear and unique and search through the name of the inventor is very simple. This type of search is done only when rival companies want to identify the areas of their competitors. However, substantive search helps in locating all the documents belonging to a given technical field. Substantive search can be made by using International Patent Classification (IPC) and database specific classification. Keywords of technical fields are also used to identify the patents in that field.

The data was processed and the above parameters were used to study different aspects of patenting activity in biosensors. Issue date was used to study the growth of patents, assignee's name was used to identify leading companies, countries name was used to identify the countries filing patents in this area of technology and by picking a keyword from the title we identified the areas where maximum patents were being field.

RESULTS

Growth in patenting Activity

The number of patents being field on biosensors has risen during 1998-11 both in absolute terms (from one in 1998-00 to 75 in 2007-09) and perhaps more importantly, as a percentage of the total number of patents filed (from 0.66% in 1998-00 to 50% in 2007-09) table 1 The sudden growth of biosensors patents during 2004-09 indicates a spurt in number of countries and companies involved in the innovative activity in this area of technology. The trend of growth clearly indicates that this is area of growing importance in scientific research.

INTER-COUNTRY COMPARISON

Table- 2 shows the number of patents for different countries and years in blocks of three years each. USA and Japan are the main patenting countries followed by UK. However, Japan was the first country to file a patent in this field.

Table 1 growth of patenting activity

Year	Number of patents filed
1998-2000	1
2001-03	6
2004-06	27
2007-09	75
2011	41
Total	150

Competitiveness among firms

By analyzing the name of the assignee author identified institutions/ firms those were filing patents in the field of biosensors. It is observed that 11 patents were individual patents and the rest 139 patents were filed by 91 institutions/ firms. Of these 139 patents, 15 patents came from academic institutions, 4 from research institutions and 12 from governmental departments.

An analysis of the growth of new companies during different periods indicates that up to 1988 only four companies have filed 7 patents, while during 2004-06 as many as 19 new companies joined the race and this number grew to 45 during 2007-

09. Further analysis of the data indicates that most of the companies active in filing patents were from USA.

Niche Areas of Patenting Activity

The data obtained for 150 patents filed in USA during 1998-00 were analyzed to identify the niche areas in which the patents were being filed. The areas in which relatively large number of patents are being filed have been considered as the niche areas. In table 3 author has listed the niche areas along with the number of patents from USA and other countries. Based on this, it is observed that enzyme membrane biosensors and electrochemical biosensors are the niche areas. Unitika Ltd and Terumo Kabushiki Kaisha, both in Japan, have been active in the area of enzyme membrane biosensors. However such an effort from companies in other countries is yet to be visible. In the field of electrochemical biosensors, Hitachi Ltd from Japan is active, while in USA the major activity in the field is in the academic and governmental research institutions.

Table-2 Distribution of patents according to patenting country

Country	Patents
USA	75
Japan	32
UK	10
Germany	6
Sweden	5
Others	22
Total	*150*

Findings

1. The number of patents in biosensors has increased both in absolute terms as well as in percentage of the total number of patents, which indicates that this is an area of growing importance in scientific research.

2. USA and Japan are the leading countries filing patents in biosensors.

3. Most of the patents are owned by industrial firms.

4. The niche area on the basis of patenting activity are enzyme membrane biosensors followed by electrochemical biosensors.

REFERENCES

1. Webster ,John G. (Editor-in-chief), Encyclopaedia of Medical Devices and Instrumentation, (John Wiley and Sons, New York) 1988.

2. Townshed, Alan (Editor-in-chief), Encyclopaedia of Analytical Science, (Academic Press, London) 1995.

3. Gupta, V.K, IPR information for R&D scientists, Journal of library and information science,26(2) 2001,114-128.

4. Arunachalam V, indigenous knowledge and IPR : the patent logistics and the overt concerns, journal of intellectual property rights, 7(3)2002,222-232.

Chapter-21

IMPORTANCE OF INTELLECTUAL PROPERTY RIGHTS IN THE BUSINESS WORLD

S.P. SHARMA AND SADHANA DIXIT*
Department of Economics, Govt. P. G. College, Morena (MP)
*Department of Hindi, Govt. P. G. College, Morena (MP)

Intellectual Property Rights are the rights given to persons over the creations of their minds. They usually give the creator an exclusive right over the use of his/her creations for a certain period of time. Intellectual Property is a term coined probably in the 19th century where its manifold applications have been projected since 20th century, commonly in the business world. Intellectual Property is a legal concept which refers to creations of the mind for which exclusive rights are recognized. Under Intellectual Property Law, owners are granted certain exclusive rights to a variety of intangible assets, such as musical, literary, and artistic works; discoveries and inventions; and words, phrases, symbols, and designs. Intellectual Property and business are two ideologies or opposite faces of the same point. It shows the inter-mingling effect of both the terms in a wider segment.

Types of IPRs

Common types of Intellectual Property Rights include patents, copy rights, industrial design rights, trade marks, trade dress and trade secrets.

Patents - A patent grants an inventor exclusive rights to make, use, sell, and import an invention for a limited period of time, in exchange for the public discloser of the invention. An invention is a solution to a specific technological problem, which may be a product or a process.

Copyright - A copyright gives the creator of an original work exclusive rights to it, usually for a limited time. Copyright may apply to a wide range of creative, Intellectual, or artistic forms, or works. Copyright does not cover ideas and information themselves, only the form or manner in which they are expressed.

Industrial Design Rights - An industrial design right protects the visual design of objects that are not purely utilitarian. An industrial design consists of the creation of a shape, configuration or composition of pattern or combination of pattern and color in three dimensional form containing aesthetic value. An industrial design can be a two-or three- dimensional pattern used to produce a product, industrial commodity or handicraft.

Trademarks - Trademarks are brand identifiers. A trademark may be any word, name , slogan, symbol, device, package design, or combination of these that serves to indentify and distinguish a product from others in the market place.

Trade dress - Trade dress is a legal term of art that generally refers to characteristics of the visual appearance of a product or its packaging that signify the source of the product to consumers.

Trade secrets - A trade secret is a formula, practice, process, design, instrument, pattern, or compilation of information which is not generally known or reasonably ascertainable, by which a business can obtain an economic advantage over competitors or customers.

Objective of IPRs

The stated objective of most Intellectual Property law is to promote progress. By exchanging limited exclusive rights for disclosure of inventions and creative works, society and patentee/copyright owner mutually benefit, and an incentive is created for inventors and authors to create and disclose their work. Some commentators have noted that the objective of Intellectual Property legislators and those who support its implementation appears to be "absolute protection". If some Intellectual Property is desirable because it encourages innovation, they reason, more is better. The thinking is that creators will not have sufficient incentive to invent unless they are legally entitled to capture the full social value of their inventions.

Relevance to Business World

Businesses need the Intellectual Property system to protect manufacturing secrets or other useful information and remain ahead of the competition. Businesses need to fully exploit their Intellectual Property assets to maintain consistent quality and market products and services to consumers so as to develop long term customer loyalty.

To remain ahead of competitors, business entitles must either continuously introduce radically new products and services or make small improvements to the quality of existing products and services. Changes are also made in response to customer needs; therefore almost every product or service used in daily life gradually evolves as a result of a series of big or small innovations, such as changes in design or improvements in a product's look and function. Businesses are also concerned with maintaining consistent quality and marketing products and services to consumers. Knowledge, both original and new, is essential to all of these processes. The Intellectual Property system is the primary key to successful management of such knowledge assets for business.

Any industry or business, whether traditional or modern, regardless of what product or service it produces or provides, is likely to regularly use Intellectual Property to prevent others from encroaching on its due reward or taking advantage of its goodwill in market. Every industry or business should systematically take the steps required for identifying, protecting and managing its Intellectual Property assets, so as to gain the best possible commercial results from its ownership.

If a business or industrial enterprise is intending to use an Intellectual Property asset belonging to someone else, it should consider buying it or acquiring the rights to use it by taking a license in order to avoid disputes and consequent expensive litigation. A business or industry could encounter legal problems for inadvertently violating the Intellectual Property rights of others out of sheer ignorance of the Intellectual Property system. Hence, a basic understanding of the Intellectual Property system has become a prerequisite for success in the marketplace.

Importance in Business World

Intellectual Property Rights are important for economists, business administrators, financial managers, managers of multinationals, international business professionals because, it offers a firm understanding of policies, rules and issues of international business. The importance of Intellectual Property Rights for the international trade and commerce has been recognized by the world over. Many international agreements to regulate grant and exploitation of Intellectual Property Right have been signed between countries of the world either bilaterally or in the form of multilateral agreements.

The days when business deals and global transactions were the territory of multinational companies are over. Now, even sole proprietors are licensed to run their own business across national boundaries. If you are interested in international business, lets move on to avail it and over come the hurdles in your business in international market. Avail this, become a successful businessman and defeat the hurdles according to the rules of international business. The use of the Intellectual Property by the society brings about social, economical, industrial and cultural prosperity in the country where such rights are granted. Industrialization has brought significant changes in the concept of property.

Business and Intellectual Property Rights provides an analytical framework for addressing legal issues and emphasises legal problem-solving through the application of prior decisions in a number of key areas of business law. The main purpose of business law is to make business deal fair and people fulfil their promises. Due to India's economic expansion, there is a strong demand for trained professionals in corporate administrative field. Knowledge in all areas of business and Intellectual Property Rights give you a competitive edge in a rapidly changing marketplace.

In today's open world there are various paths leading to inventions and discoveries by every day. With the competition being faced today, by projecting your superiority in creative ideologies is gaining an upper foot-hold in business plays a vital role in the ethics and the economics of any venture. Running a successful business with current and inventive ideas today is actively attacked by competitions. To me this is the juncture where the Intellectual Property Rights come into play by safeguarding the creativeness of any business.

It has been observed from close quarters that running a successful business always depends upon original ideas with existing trends. At this point of view there may be inter-mingling, copying, over-treading the visions created by someone else. This may be done by business houses knowingly or unknowingly with profit as the ultimate aim. Here in the Intellectual Property Rights is landed. In the broader spectrum, the Intellectual Property Rights safeguards or acts as a binder to the creator of ideas in a particular sector or field wherein these rights binds the maker with the creation lawfully, wherein infringement can be considered unlawful.

Intellectual Property Rights come into play whenever any creation is used for economic gains or a public display to protect the strings of the creation. Intellectual Property Rights assist the business in all spheres of development and strategies adopted in expanding the business. The forms of Intellectual Property allow you and your products to be distinguished individually from others. They are a seal of authority in the respect to the quality, product, services and expectations put forth by the buyer or the user. Intellectual Property helps a business in distinguishing him from others for higher profit margins.

This way the Intellectual Property Rights is co-related in safeguarding, enhancing and developing business possibilities.

REFERENCES

1. Brenkert , George G., Oxford Handbook of Business Ethics.

2. Lee, Richmond K., Scope and Interplay of IP Rights.

3. Small Business Bible: The importance of trade mark in a small business setup.

4. www.wipo.sme.

Chapter-22

INTELLECTUAL PROPERTY RIGHT (IPR): AN INTRODUCTION

MRIDUL PRATEEK SINGH

NATIONAL LAW UNIVERSITY, VISHAKHAPATNAM

Intellectual Property Right (IPR) is a term used for various legal entitlements which attach to certain types of information, ideas, or other intangibles in their expressed form. The holder of this legal entitlement is generally entitled to exercise various exclusive rights in relation to the subject matter of the Intellectual Property. The term intellectual property reflects the idea that this subject matter is the product of the mind or the intellect, and that Intellectual Property Rights may be protected at law in the same way as any other form of property. Intellectual Property laws vary from jurisdiction to jurisdiction, such that the acquisition, registration or enforcement of IP rights must be pursued or obtained separately in each territory of interest.

INTRODUCTION

Intellectual property rights (IPR) can be defined as the rights given to people over the creation of their minds. They usually give the creator an exclusive right over the use of his/her creations for a certain period of time. Intellectual property is an intangible creation of the human mind, usually expressed or translated into a tangible form that is assigned certain rights of property. Examples of intellectual property include an author's copyright on a book or article, a distinctive logo design representing a soft drink company and its products, unique design elements of a web site, or a patent on the process to manufacture chewing gum.

Intellectual property rights (IPR) can be defined as the rights given to people over the creation of their minds. They usually give the creator an exclusive right over the use of his/her creations for a certain period of time.

Intellectual property (IP) refers to creations of the mind: inventions, literary and artistic works Intellectual property (IP) refers to creations of the mind: inventions, literary and artistic works.

HISTORY

Modern usage of the term *intellectual property* goes back at least as far as 1867 with the founding of the North German Confederation whose constitution granted legislative power over the protection of intellectual property to the confederation. When the administrative secretariats established by the Paris Convention (1883) and the Berne Convention (1886) merged in 1893, they located in Berne, and also adopted the term intellectual property in their new combined title, the United International Bureaux for the Protection of Intellectual Property.

The organisation subsequently relocated to Geneva in 1960, and was succeeded in 1967 with the establishment of the World Intellectual Property Organization (WIPO) by treaty as an agency of the United Nations. According to Lemley, it was only at this point that the term really began to be used in the United States (which had not been a party to the Berne Convention), and it did not enter popular usage until passage of the Bayh-Dole Act in 1980.

"The history of patents does not begin with inventions, but rather with royal grants by Queen Elizabeth I (1558-1603) for monopoly privileges. Approximately 200 years after the end of Elizabeth's reign, however, a patent represents a legal [right] obtained by an inventor providing for exclusive control over the production and sale of his mechanical or scientific invention. [demonstrating] the evolution of patents from royal prerogative to common-law doctrine

In an 1818 collection of his writings, the French liberal theorist, Benjamin Constant, argued against the recently introduced idea of "property which has been called intellectual." The term *intellectual property* can be found used in an October 1845 Massachusetts Circuit Court ruling in the patent case *Davoll et al.* v. Brown., in which Justice Charles L. Woodbury wrote that "only in this way can we protect intellectual property, the labors of the mind, productions and interests are as much a man's own...as the wheat he cultivates, or the flocks he rears." The statement that "discoveries are...property" goes back earlier. Section 1 of the French law of 1791 stated, "All new discoveries are the property of the author; to assure the inventor the property and temporary enjoyment of his discovery, there shall be delivered to him a patent for five, ten orfifteen years." In Europe, French author A. Nion mentioned *propriété intellectuelle* in his Droits civils des auteurs, artistes et *inventeurs*, published in 1846.

Until recently, the purpose of intellectual property law was to give as little protection possible in order to encourage innovation. Historically, therefore, they were granted only when they were necessary to encourage invention, limited in time and scope.

The concept's origins can potentially be traced back further. Jewish law includes several considerations whose effects are similar to those of modern intellectual property laws, though the notion of intellectual creations as property does not seem to exist - notably the principle of Hasagat Ge'vul (unfair encroachment) was used to justify limited-term publisher (but not author) copyright in the 16th century. In 500 BCE, the government of the Greek state of Sybaris offered one year's patent "to all who should discover any new refinement in luxury.

WHY INTELLECTUAL PROPERTY IS IMPORTANT ?

For business

In today's world, the abundant supply of goods and services on the markets has made life very challenging for any business, big or small. In its on-going quest to remain ahead of competitors in this environment, every business strives to create new and improved products (goods and services) that will deliver greater value to users and customers than the products offered by competitors. To differentiate their products - a prerequisite for success in today's markets - businesses rely on innovations that reduce production costs and/or improve product quality. In a crowded marketplace, businesses have to make an on-going effort to communicate the specific value Offered by their product through effective marketing that relies on well thought-out branding strategies.

In the current knowledge-driven, private sector oriented economic development paradigm, the different types of intangible assets of a business are often more important and valuable than its tangible assets. A key subset of intangible assets is protected by what are labelled collectively as intellectual property rights (IPRs). These include trade secrets protection, copyright, design and trademark rights, and patents, as well as other types of rights. IPRs create tradable assets out of products of human intellect, and provide a large array of IPR tools on which businesses can rely to help drive their success through innovative business models All businesses, especially those which are already successful, nowadays have to rely on the effective use of one or more types of intellectual property (IP) to gain and maintain a substantial competitive edge in the marketplace. Business leaders and managers, therefore, require a much better understanding of the tools of the IP system to protect and exploit the IP assets they own, or wish to use, for their business models and competitive strategies in domestic and international markets.

IPRs provide a basis for businesses to

1. prevent others from copying their products or using their innovations - this is particularly relevant in today's competitive markets

2. create a strong brand identity - by product differentiation through the strategic use of one or more types of IPRs

3. obtain valuable competitive intelligence - analysing commercial and technological information from patent, trademark and design databases can increase a company's understanding of technological fields and trends; identify future research and growth areas; and analyse competitors, thereby saving research/development/ marketing time and resources;

4. gain revenues through licensing, franchising or other IP transactions;

5. obtain financing or venture capital - IP assets which have legal protection and can be valued can be leveraged to obtain capital,

6. engage in different types of business partnerships - IP rights provide a basis for collaborative partnerships.

The role IP plays in a business can vary depending on different factors such as:

1. The business model - some models will have IP as a key element while IP may play a less central role in other models. Different types of IPRs will also be relevant to different business models e.g. patents, know-how and trade secrets will be central to technology companies, while trademarks and designs will be more important to consumer brand sector;

2. The type of IP used - different types of IPRs play different roles (e.g. trademark protection

3. will be used to protect brands; patents to protect technology copyright to protect software; design rights to protect new designs). Most businesses will utilize more than one type of IPR

4. The stage of the business' evolution: the role of IPRs in a business will usually become more sophisticated as the business evolves

The awareness of its managers about the role of IP: the importance given to in a business will depend on how its managers approach the IP function

IMPORTANCE OF IPR IN RESEARCH

Innovation and IP are separate concepts but closely-linked. Innovation often leads to the creation of IP, and IPRs help provide a vehicle to obtain the financing to develop innovative ideas and to move them into the market. Innovation should not be an end in itself but should be methodically integrated into business culture and practices to enhance overall performance. Innovation can be integrated into all areas of business as follows

A company's ability to innovate is crucial to maintaining competitiveness in today's increasingly globalized markets. While competing on price may suffice in the short term, such competitive advantage is unsustainable over a long period. Sustained competitive advantage requires constant innovation in both production and management. However the ability to generate innovation on a consistent basis requires a paradigmatic shift in the workplace culture. Business membership organizations are well-placed to provide businesses with the requisite skill sets and tools to foster sustained innovation processes have changed rapidly in recent years, largely as a result of advances in the area of information technologies and communication technologies (ICT) and the high level of global economic integration. These two factors have accelerated and transformed ways of generating and transferring knowledge and technology Integrating innovation into an overall business strategy and as a work method will increase market competitiveness. As this is difficult in practice, member companies of business membership organizations will greatly benefit from specific services in this field. These can include advice on how to innovate on a sustainable basis, including assessments of individual companies, as well as the publication of reports and studies.

CONCLUSION

Most IP policy measures will have a direct impact on some or all sectors of businesses Individual companies look to their trade associations or business organizations to represent their views to policy makers for several reasons: collective views carry more weight than the voice of one company; most companies do not have the resources to engage in policy advocacy activities; and policy makers often find it easier to engage with a single representative organization which has already defined a consensus industry view rather than with many individual companies.

Engaging in policy discussions on IP will enhance the business membership organization's leadership role in this area, and raise its profile among both the business community and policy makers. As IP is a horizontal, cross-cutting issue that relates to most other policy areas, it is useful for business membership organizations to have defined their IP positions when engaging in related discussions.

REFERENCES

1. HASTING LAW JOURNAL Vol. 52 PG -1255.

2. Property as a common descriptor of the field probably traces to the foundation of the world intellectual property organization (WIPO).

3. Sherman, Brad, The making of modern intellectual property law

4. Yu, Peter. 2007 Intellectual Property and wealth.

5. Arai, Hisamitsu. "Intellectual Property Policies for the Twenty-First Century: The Japanese Experience in Wealth Creation", WIPO Publication Number 834 (E). 2000.

6. Hahn, Robert W., *Intellectual Property Rights in Frontier Industries.*

7. De George, Richard T. "14. Intellectual Property Rights." In The Oxford *Handbook of Business Ethics,* by George G. Brenkert and Tom L.

8. IP Management for enhancing the competitiveness of SME'S.

9. The Role of Intellectual Property Rights in the Promotion of Competitiveness.

Chapter-23

IPR AND PROTECTION OF PLANT VARIETIES

RAJDEEP KUDESIA

Department of Botany, Bundelkhand University, Jhansi (U.P.) India

IPR is a general term that includes patents, Copyright, trademark, industrial designs, geographical indications, protection of layout designs of integrated circuits and protection of undisclosed information.

In India Patents, designs, trademarks and geographical indications are administered by the Controller general of patents, Designs and Trademark. Which is under the control of The Department of Industrial Policy and Promotion, Ministry of Commerce and Industry. Copyright is under the charge of the Ministry of Human Resource Development. The Act on Layout Design of Integrated circuits will be implemented by the Ministry of Communication and Information Technology.

There are two basic limitations of patents (1) It is for a limited time. (2) A patent is valid only in the country of its award but not in other countries but when the patent is awarded by WTO it is valid in all countries that are members of WTO.

A plant variety is developed and released after performing many tedious exercises by a person and a group of persons. Therefore it should be considered as Intellectual Property of the Breeder who has developed it. Many countries consider plant varieties as an Intellectual Property and grant a protection through Patent. A large number of countries follow UPOV 1991Act to protect the newly developed varieties. India give protection to plant varieties through Protection of Plant Varieties and Farmer's Right Act 2001 (PPV&FR Act-2001).

UPOV 1991 Act: According to rules and regulations of UPOV 1991 Act a plant variety will be protected if it satisfies its novelty, distinctiveness, uniformity and stability. There are following main provisions in this act-

The holder of the PBR title will have the right for commercial production and sale of germplasm.

(A) A farmer (or grower) can keep some germplasm for next year's production but not allowed for selling at commercial level it is called farmer's right

(B) Breeding methods are not protected under PBR

(C) Exchange of germplasm between cultivars is not allowed

(D) Developed variety will be protected for a limited period (minimum 20 years)

(E) PBR protects new varieties but not its pedigree

(F) The protected cultivar may be used for developing genetic variability without permission of title holder

Table-1   MEMBERS OF THE INTERNATIONAL UNION FOR THE PROTECTION OF NEW VARIETIES OF PLANTS.

International Convention for the Protection of New Varieties of Plants*UPOV Convention (1961), as revised at Geneva (1972, 1978 and 1991) Status on December 5, 2012

State/ Organization	Date on which State/Organization became member of UPOV	Number of contribution units	Latest Act[1] of the Convention to which State/Organization is party and date on which State/Organization became party to that Act		
Albania	October 15, 2005	0.2	1991	Act	October 15, 2005
Argentina	December 25, 1994	0.5	1978	Act	December 25, 1994
Australia	March 1, 1989	1.0	1991	Act	January 20, 2000
Austria	July 14, 1994	0.75	1991	Act	July 1, 2004
Azerbaijan	December 9, 2004	0.2	1991	Act	December 9, 2004
Belarus	January 5, 2003	0.2	1991	Act	January 5, 2003
Belgium 2	December 5, 1976	1.5	1961/1972	Act	December 5, 1976
Bolivia	May 21, 1999	0.2	1978	Act	.May 21, 1999
Brazil	May 23, 1999	0.25	1978	Act	May 23, 1999
Bulgaria	April 24, 1998	0.2	1991	Act	April 24, 1998
Canada	March 4, 1991	1.0	1978	Act	March 4, 1991
Chile	January 5, 1996	0.2	1978	Act	January 5, 1996
China	April 23, 1999	0.5	1978	Act 3	April 23, 1999
Colombia	September 13, 1996	0.2	1978	Act	September 13, 1996
Costa Rica	January 12, 2009	0.2	1991	Act	January 12, 2009
Croatia	September 1, 2001	0.2	1991	Act	September 1, 2001
Czech Republic	January 1, 1993	0.5	1991	Act	November 24, 2002
Denmark 4	October 6, 1968	0.5	1991	Act	April 24, 1998
Dominican Republic	June 16, 2007	0.2	1991	Act	June 16, 2007
Ecuador	August 8, 1997	0.2	1978	Act	August 8, 1997
Estonia	September 24, 2000	0.2	1991	Act	September 24, 2000
European Union	July 29, 2005	5.0	1991	Act	July 29, 2005
Finland	April 16, 1993	1.0	1991	Act	July 20, 2001

Contd.....

Table-1 Contd....

France	October 3, 1971	5.0	1991	Act	May 27, 2012
Georgia	November 29, 2008	0.2	1991	Act	November 29, 2008
Germany	August 10, 1968	5.0	1991	Act	July 25, 1998
Hungary	April 16, 1983	0.5	1991	Act	January 1, 2003
Iceland	May 3, 2006	0.2	1991	Act	May 3, 2006
Ireland	November 8, 1981	1.0	1991	Act	January 8, 2012
Israel	December 12, 1979	0.5	1991	Act	April 24, 1998
Italy	July 1, 1977	2.0	1978	Act	May 28, 1986
Japan	September 3, 1982	5.0	1991	Act	December 24, 1998
Jordan	October 24, 2004	0.2	1991	Act	October 24, 2004
Kenya	May 13, 1999	0.2	1978	Act	May 13, 1999
Kyrgyzstan	June 26, 2000	0.2	1991	Act	June 26, 2000
Latvia	August 30, 2002	0.2	1991	Act	August 30, 2002
Lithuania	December 10, 2003	0.2	1991	Act	December 10, 2003
Mexico	August 9, 1997	0.75	1978	Act	August 9, 1997
Morocco	October 8, 2006	0.2	1991	Act	October 8, 2006
Netherlands	August 10, 1968	3.0	1991	Act 5	April 24, 1998
New Zealand	November 8, 1981	1.0	1978	Act	November 8, 1981
Nicaragua	September 6, 2001	0.2	1978	Act	September 6, 2001
Norway	September 13, 1993	1.0	1978	Act	September 13, 1993
Oman	November 22, 2009	1.0	1991	Act	November 22, 2009
Panama	May 23, 1999	0.2	1991	Act	November 22, 2012
Paraguay	February 8, 1997	0.2	1978	Act	February 8, 1997
Peru	August 8, 2011	0.2	1991	Act	August 8, 2011
Poland	November 11, 1989	0.5	1991	Act	August 15, 2003
Portugal	October 14, 1995	0.2	1978	Act	October 14, 1995
Republic of Korea	January 7, 2002	1.5	1991	Act	January 7, 2002
Republic of Moldova	October 28, 1998	0.2	1991	Act	October 28, 1998
Romania	March 16, 2001	0.2	1991	Act	March 16, 2001
Russian Federation	April 24, 1998	0.5	1991	Act	April 24, 1998
Serbia	January 5, 2013	0.2	1991	Act	January 5, 2013
Singapore	July 30, 2004	0.2	1991	Act	July 30, 2004
Slovakia	January 1, 1993	0.5	1991	Act	June 12, 2009
Slovenia	July 29, 1999	0.2	1991	Act	July 29, 1999
South Africa	November 6, 1977	1.0	1978	Act	November 8, 1981
Spain	May 18, 1980	2.0	1991	Act	July 18, 2007
Sweden	December 17, 1971	1.5	1991	Act	April 24, 1998
Switzerland	July 10, 1977	1.5	1991	Act	September 1, 2008

Contd.....

Table-1 Contd....

The former Yugoslav Republic					
of Macedonia	May 4, 2011	0.2	1991	Act	May 4, 2011
Trinidad and					
Tobago	January 30, 1998	0.2	1978	Act	January 30, 1998
Tunisia	August 31, 2003	0.2	1991	Act	August 31, 2003
Turkey	November 18, 2007	0.5	1991	Act	November 18, 2007
Ukraine	November 3, 1995	0.2	1991	Act	January 19, 2007
United Kingdom	August 10, 1968	2.0	1991	Act	January 3, 1999
United States of					
America	November 8, 1981	5.0	1991	Act 6	February 22, 1999
Uruguay	November 13, 1994	0.2	1978	Act	November 13, 1994
Uzbekistan	November 14, 2004	0.2	1991	Act .	November 14, 2004
Viet Nam	December 24, 2006	0.2	1991	Act	December 24, 2006

* The International Union for the Protection of New Varieties of Plants (UPOV), established by the International Convention for the Protection of New Varieties of Plants, is an independent intergovernmental organization having legal personality. Pursuant to an agreement concluded between the World Intellectual Property Organization (WIPO) and UPOV, the Director General of WIPO is the Secretary-General of UPOV and WIPO provides administrative services to UPOV.

1 "1961/1972 Act" means the International Convention for the Protection of New Varieties of Plants of December 2, 1961, as amended by the Additional Act of November 10, 1972; "1978 Act" means the Act of October 23, 1978, of the Convention; "1991 Act" means the Act of March 19, 1991, of the Convention.

2 With a notification under Article 34(2) of the 1978 Act.

3 With a declaration that the 1978 Act is not applicable to Hong Kong, China.

4 With a declaration that the Convention of 1961, the Additional Act of 1972, the 1978 Act and the 1991 Act are not applicable to Greenland and the Faroe Islands.

5 Ratification for the Kingdom in Europe.

6 With a reservation pursuant to Article 35(2) of the 1991 Act.

India provides protection to plant varieties through Protection of Plant Varieties and Farmer's Right Act 2001(PPV&FR ACT-2001)

For the protection of plant varieties in India Protection of Plant Varieties &Farmer's Right Act (2001) was passed on 9th August 2001 in Lok Sabha. The key features of the Act are as follows-

1.   A new variety which has been set for registration must satisfy the criteria of novelty, distinctiveness, uniformity and stability.

2.   Farmer's varieties, extant varieties and new varieties may be registered.

3.   Any variety that is injurious to life of human being, animals or existing varieties will not be registered.

4. Essentially derived variety(variety derived from initial variety) can also be registeredas a new variety.

5. The time period of protection of the varieties will be 15 years except varieties of trees (where it is 18 years).

6. The breeder or his successor will have full right to produce, sell, distribute and export of the variety.

7. A researcher may use the variety for research purpose without paying any royalty to the PBR title holder.

8. The Act also recognizes farmer's rights.

9. The Central government is to constitute a National Gene Fund from the earnings of benefit sharing of registered varieties, compensations deposited in the fund and contributions from National and International organizations.

10. The Central government will establish the Protection of Plant Varieties and Farmer's Right Authority (PPVFRA). In India PPVFRA has been established on 11th November 2007.

11. The Central government shall establish a Plant Varieties Registry for the registration of plant varieties.

12. The breeder shall be required to submit a specified quantities of germplasm of registered variety as well as its parental lines in the National Gene Bank.

The Protection of Plant Varieties and Farmers' Right Act 2001 (PPV&FR Act) has been implemented in India. The Rules came into existence from 7th December 2006. The purpose of the Act is to provide an effective system for protection of plant varieties, recognize the rights of farmers and plant breeders and to encourage the development of new varieties of plants.

The Indian Act is unique as it not only provides for protection of breeders but also takes care of the farmers' rights as well as the Rights of the Communities, Researcher's Rights, Benefit Sharing and Compulsory Licensing.

According to the Protection of Plant Varieties and Farmers' Rights Act, 2001, under section 14 an application for registration of a new variety extant variety and farmer's variety can be filed by (a) any person claiming to be the breeder of the variety; or (b) any successor of the breeder; or (c) any person being the assignee of the breeder of the variety in respect of the right to make such application; or (d) any farmer or group of farmers or community of farmers claiming to be the breeder of the variety; (e) any person authorized in the prescribed manner (f) any university or publicly funded agricultural institution claiming to be the breeder of the variety.

Process of Registration of Plant Variety in India

Registration of plant varieties can be made in the office of Registrar, PPV&FRA, New Delhi. The address of the Office is: Registrar, Protection of Plant Varieties and Farmers' Rights Authority, Govt. of India, Ministry of Agriculture, NASC Complex, DPS Marg, Opposite Todapur, New Delhi - 110 012 and the process of registration may be summarized as follows:

Application for new variety 1. Form I - for registration of new variety, extant variety and farmer's variety and 2 Form II - for essentially derived varieties (EDVs) and transgenic varieties.

⇓

Checking of its Novelty. Distinctiveness, Uniformity and Stability under section 19 0f PPV&FR

⇓

Either the application will be accepted under section 20(2) of the Act or rejected after providing an opportunity of hearing

⇓

Application is published in the Plant variety Journal for opposition within three months

⇓

If no opposition is filed to the published variety ,variety will be registered

Plant Breeder's Right (PBR) These rights are granted by a government to a plant breeder of a variety to restrict others from producing or use it for commercial purpose for at least 15-18 years but it does not protect breeding procedure that is used to develop a variety. A person holding PBR title to a variety can authorize other interested person to produce and market propagating material of that variety after setting some reasonable terms for such transfer of PBR titles. PBR systems also have some form of "breeder's exemption" and "farmer's privilege".

Breeder's Exemption: The registered variety may be used by otherbreeder fo the development of new variety without giving any royalty to the title holder, it is called breeder's exemption.

Farmer's Privilege: PBR systems allow farmers to use the material of protected variety for planting of their new crop without paying any royalty to the PBR title holder, this is called Farmer's privilege.

Farmers' Rights

1. Farmer who has bred or developed a new variety shall be entitled for registration and other protection under PPV&FR Act, 2001 in the same manner as a breeder of a variety.

2. If he is engaged in the conservation of genetic resources of land races and wild relatives of economic plants and their improvement through selection and preservation shall be entitled in the prescribed manner for recognition and reward from the Gene Fund provided that material so selected and preserved has been used as donors of genes in varieties registered under this act.

3. He will be entitled to save, use, sow, re-sow, exchange and share or sell his farm produce including seed of a variety protected under this act in the same manner as he was entitled before the coming into force of this act provided that the farmer shall not be entitled to sell branded seed of a variety protected under this Act.

What Types of New Varieties can not be registered?

Section 15 (4) of the Act deals with New Varieties which cannot be registered under the Act. This provision is more like Section 3 of the Patent Act which is in the nature of prohibitory provision. Thus any application for New Variety has to withstand the tests laid down under section 15 (4) of the Act in order to be registered, subject to other provisions of the Act and the mandatory test under Section 19 of the Act.

A New Variety shall not be registered if the denomination given to the variety is not capable of indentifying such variety; or

A New Variety shall not be registered under the provisions of the Act if the denomination given to such variety is not capable of identifying such variety or consists of solely of figures or is liable to mislead or to cause confusion concerning the characteristic, value identity of such variety or the identity of breeder of such variety; or

A New Variety shall also not be registered if it is not different from every denomination which designates a variety of the same botanical species or of a closely related species registered under the Act; or

A New Variety shall also not be registered under the Act if it is likely to deceive the public or cause confusion in the public regarding the identity of such variety; or

A New Variety is also not entitled to be registered if it is likely to hurt the religious sentiments of any class or section of the citizens of India or is prohibited for use as a name or emblem and names or is comprised solely or partly of geographical names; or

A New Variety or Extant Variety shall also not be registered if it contains any gene or gene sequence involving any harmful technology including terminator technology which is injurious to the life or health of human beings, animals or plants.

The Registrar may register a New Variety under the Act, if the denomination given to such variety comprises solely or partly of geographical name, if he considers that the usage of such denomination is an honest use under the circumstances of the Case.

The Act mandates that every new variety subject to the criteria of Novelty, Distinctiveness, uniformity an stability shall be registered under the Act.

REFERENCES:

1. http://www.patent info.net
2. http://www.infijuridique.com
3. http://www.info.org.in
4. http://www. Wipo.int
5. Singh, B.D. (2012). Plant Breeding, Principles and Methods, Kalyani Publishers, New Delhi, India
6. TIFAC, New Delhi

Chapter-24

ROLE OF IPR IN BIOTECHNOLOGY

MUKULITA UPADHYAY AND SHOBHITA UPADHYAY*

Department of Zoology, Govt. P. G. College, Morena (MP)
*Department of English, Govt. Model Science College, Gwalior (MP)

IPR refers to the legal ownership of an invention by its inventor which protects him against unauthorized copying. Field of Biotechnology is an upcoming science which promises a revolution in the field of pharmaceuticals, agriculture, medicine and industrial sectors. IPRs are intended primarily to foster private R & D and to encourage access to invention produced elsewhere. The functioning of intellectual property rights in the field of Biotechnology had become necessary so as to safe guard the rights of the inventor and to encourage and promote invention and innovations which can be a boon for the economy.

The Indian Biotechnology sector has shown tremendous growth in the last decade. Due to fast growing developments the power of IPR has grown. Now the people have the option of licensing research outputs. These outputs are the result of tremendous research, labour and require huge investments hence IPR is an effective tool to protect biotechnology inventions.

IPR AND BIOTECHNOLOGY INDUSTRY

Processes and products are the main features of Intellectual property in the field of Bio-technology. These products and processes are the result of genetic engineering techniques. These researches under the hold of IPRs would encourage the industries to establish research and development units and would provide funds for commercially marketable items.

Intellectual Property (IP) is central to the biotechnology industry whether it is related to drug discovery, clinical or market related trials. The successful translation of these innovations into commercially viable application and marketable products depend on the registration and its legal protection as intellectual property.

IPR has made private enterprise possible in many broad research areas in agriculture and health science. Over the past decade, India has shown excellence in scientific performance in terms of the number and quantity of publication made each year in international journals. In spite of excellent work its commercial and technological performance is low due to the fact that a very less number of patents have been issued per unit of investments.

FORMS OF IPR IN BIOTECHNOLOGY

(1) Patent

It is a form of IPR which acts as a balance between the investor and the state (National government). Patent may be defined as "Exclusive rights given by the state to its inventor in exchange for a public discloser of an invention for a fixed time period. This rights would exclude others from using, making or selling the invention. Patent law exists is over 100 countries. In some countries patent for genetic material both plant and animal have been allowed. The patented material can never be used further for breeding without paying a fee to the patent holders. Biotechnology patent applications experience numerous restrictions due to undefined scope & complex nature of the technology. Article 27 of TRIPS agreement clearly defines the guidelines in making distinction between material produced by biological processes and by non biological methods. Natural material of any kind is not patentable and it has been made clear that the member state should exclude animals and plants from patentability. Microorganism have scope of patentability . There are also controversies against patenting life form like transgenic animals and plants.

(2) Copyrights

Copyrights are the set of rights given to the creator or the author of original work. It includes edited books, research papers, cassettes both audio and video etc. The publisher author or editor holds the copyright and nobody can reproduce his work without his consent. Reproducing his exclusive work without his permission is considered as illegal and comes under the category of punishable offense. In the field of Biotechnology copyrights cover computer databases, DNA sequence data and photo micrographics of DNA instruction manuals.

(3) Trade Marks

Trademarks are the reservation of a word, symbol or phrase in association with a product. It is used by the manufacturer for his products which makes it different from those manufactured by others. In the field of Biotechnology the laboratory instruments and equipments holds trademarks. Vectors used in the recombinant DNA technology is generally known by their trademarks.

(4) Trade secrets

There is no international tabulation of trade secret legislation. It includes any physical material or any private information related to any property that has an advantage to its owner. In the area of biotechnology trade secrets includes F1 hybrids with in agriculture, cell lines, customer lists, corporate merchandising plans etc.

(5) Plant Breeder' s right (PBR)

It is a specialized patent like system for cultivated plants, In industrialized countries crop varieties are subjected to intellectual property rights in the form of PBR. PBR's are distinguished from patents as these rights are "farmers privilege". The farmers have the privilege of the right to hold the materials for subsequent seasons. PBR also guarantees the "research exemption" acc to which the protected material can be used for developing a new variety or other research use.

INTELLECTUAL PROPERTY REGULATIONS IN BIOTECHNOLOGY

TRIP is an international treaty which along with WTO provides a foundation for IPR protection but its enforcement is lacking in many parts of the world. The products and processes are patentable if they meet three criteria - being novel, involving an inventive step and being capable of Industrial application. Biotechnology patent applications has number of restrictions due to undefined scope and complex nature of the technology.

IPR protection is granted only for inventions and not for discoveries so at times it becomes difficult to decide whether a new life form in the form of a cell or DNA is a technological invention or a scientific discovery. Next, it raises important policy questions such as degree to which private ownership could be granted to an innovator. Article 27 of TRIPS agreement makes it clear that plants and animals should be excluded from the scope of patentability. However, it is unclear whether biological substances like genes and cells are excluded or not. TRIPs provide option to the member states protecting new plant varieties by means of patents or suigeneris. Plant variety protection boosts the research work by both public & private bodies. The "intellectual property rights" grant patents to private corporations but the traditional knowledge is not legally protected as intellectual property.

It is exploited by Modern Science and Industry without adequate recompense to the indigenizes and local communities that are the custodians of the knowledge. By such system only private industries and the multinational corporation are benefited.

Biopiracy of genetics resources and traditional knowledge is on increase. In India, most of the pharmaceutical applications are based on ayurvedic knowledge. Many of these clams with minor modifications in methods of extraction and processing could amount to biopiracy. The developed countries and there multinational corporation are the main users of patent protection. Since the over whelming proportions of patent originate in the developed countries, patent protection lead to transfer of income from less developed countries to developed countries and would thereby widen income disparities between the two. In some developed countries like U.S. the patent applicants face problems with the inability of the U.S. Patent and Trademark Office (USPTO) to examine biotechnology or pharmaceutical inventions in a single patent application. So the applicants are forced to divide the technology into several different inventions only one of which could be pursued in the original application due to lack of funds for the complete coverage of their inventions the development of a therapeutic or diagnostic product is delayed. Currently efforts are being made to reform this administrative process so as to improve the patent quality and efficiency.

Biotechnology is considered to be the science of 21st Century. An efficient, patent protection along with industry's maturing relationship with the capital markets can serve as the hallmarks for any country to become a global leader of this technology. But since most developing countries have weak IPR regimes and lack of effective copyright laws so they suffer a lot. Scientists and technician are forced to immigrate to countries where their research is protected by illegal exploitation. The improved patent laws can bring about tremendous growth in both investments and research and development (R & D).

REFERENCES

1. Trehan , Keshav, (1990). Biotechnology Wiley Eastern Ltd.

2. Sreenivasulu, N.S. (2006). Intellectual Property Rights, Regal publications, New Delhi, India.

3. Abbott, F.M. (1998). The Enduring Enigma of TRIPS : A challenge for the world Economic System.

4. Journal of International Economic Law (1998).

5. www.patent office.nic.in

6. www.wipo.net

Chapter-25

RELEVANCE AND AWARENESS TO IPR IN INDIA

AKHILESH CHANDRA RAGHUVANSHI

Department of Botany,
S.M.S. Govt. Model Science College, Gwalior (MP)

Intellectual property refers to creation of human mind and Intellectual Property Rights are the rights given to a person or groups for their creation over the use of the other for a certain period of time. According to World Intellectual Property Organization (WIPO) convention: Article 2(viii) "intellectual property shall include rights relating to

- literary, artistic and scientific works,

- performances of performing artists, phonograms and broadcasts,

- inventions in all fields of human endeavor,

- scientific discoveries,

- industrial designs,

- trademarks, service marks and commercial names and designations,

- protection against unfair competition,

and all other rights resulting from intellectual activity in the industrial, scientific, literary or artistic fields.

Intellectual Property Laws in India

Indian Trade and Merchandise The majority of countries in the word have a system of Intellectual Property protection and enforcement. The Intellectual Property Rights (IPR) laws in India were imported from the west. The first Patent law in India was passed in 1856. The First law related to with IPR was Indian Trade and Merchandise Mark Act 1884. After independence earlier laws were changed and named as Mark Act 1958 and Copyright Act 1957. IPR related issue in India like Patents, Trademarks, Copyrights, Design and Geographical indications are governed by Indian patent Act 1970 and Patent Rules 2003, Trademark Act 1199 and the Trademark Rules 2002, Indian Copyright Act 1957 Semicondctor Integrated Circuits Layout Design Act 2000 and Rules 2001, The Geographical Indication of Goods (Registration and Protection) Rules 2002 &2005 and Protection of Plant Varieties & Farmer's Right Act 001.

The principles on which the patent laws and system are based giving exclusive rights to inventor are:

- It encourage research and invention

- Induces an inventor to disclose his/her discoveries

- Generate capital for new research and development

- Offers reward for expenses of developing inventions

The Government of India considering globalised scenario of expanding multilateral trade and commerce has taken a comprehensive sets of initiative to streamline the intellectual property administration. Under the Ministry of Commerce and Industry, the office of Controller General o of Patents, Design and Trade Marks (CGPTM) has been setup. It administers all matters relating to patents, design, trademarks and geographical indications and also supervise the functioning of The Patent Office(Including Design Wing),The Patent Information System(PIS),The Trade Marks Registry (TMR) and The Geographical Indications Registry. A Copy Rights Office has been setup in the Department of MHRD, to provide all facility including registration of copyrights and its neighbouring rights. Department of Information Technology in is nodal organization to deal issues of Layout design of integrated circuits.

International IPR regime

The majority of countries in the world have a system of intellectual property protection and enforcement laws, because it encourages innovation and creativity which ultimately leads to prosperity of a nation. Patent have a territorial effect. There is no "World Patent" to give protection to worldwide.

The first known laws regarding IPR was passed in 15th century in Venice in 1447. The law protects the investor's interest against copying of their creation. However the intellectual property system as we know today was created at various congresses in Vienna and rest of Europe. With Paris convention for the Protection of Industrial property in 1883.The three main rights *viz*. Patents, Trade Marks & Industrial design were granted protection in Paris Convention. The Paris convention made it easier for individuals in one nation to obtain protection globally .India became the member of this convention in 1998The convention was followed by Berne convention for protection of literacy & Artistic Works.

The General Agreement on Tariff and Trade (GATT) came in existence in 1949 during UN conference on Trade and Employment and lasted till 1993, it was later replaced by World Trade Organisation in 1995. This organization became an international forum to discuss the understanding and development of IPRs as successor of GATT. During various round of discussions the main concern of developing countries over the international market, multinational corporations (MNCs) and great disparity between developed and developing countries were discussed. The organization main aim was to maximize the trade, investment and development opportunity and business prospects of developing countries and also help these nation to integrate into the world economy on equitable basis. When Trade Related Intellectual Property Rights (TRIPS) came into force in January 1995, it lays down minimum standard for protection and enforcement of intellectual property rights in member countries which are required to promote effective and adequate protection of IPRs with a view to reducing distortion and impediments to international trade.

Concern and Objection to IP Laws

There has been some criticism to IPR and related laws and its impact on developing countries especially in India. IPR have never been economically and politically important or controversial than they are today. Developing countries like India went along with TRIPS agreement for a variety of reasons, ranging from the hope of additional access to agricultural market and apparel market in rich nations. There are expectation that a stronger IPR regime would encourage additional Technology transfer and innovation. However, the promising long term benefit are uncertain and costly in many nation especially in very poor countries. Some point out that, in modern economy the minimum standard laid down in TRIPS will bring benefit to developing countries by creating the incentive structure necessary for knowledge generation and diffusion, technology transfer and private investment flows .Some thought that patenting regime will adversely affect the pursuit of sustainable development strategies by raising the price of essential drugs to level that are too high for the poor to afford . It would also limit the educational materials to developing countries at school and university level, legitimizing the piracy of Traditional Knowledge (TK) and undermining the self reliance of resource to poor farmers.

Protection of Traditional Knowledge

The term Traditional Knowledge means that the knowledge being held with the indigenous, local, and traditional people or community in their use of natural and cultural resources. There is difference of opinion at the bringing of TK under IPR & TRIPS. In India no laws or act has been framed to legalize the TK. There is problem in regards to Biological Diversity, plant varieties protection& geographical indication in the implementation phase of these grey areas related to ownership issue, prior informed consent (PIC), material transfer , access and benefit sharing (ABS). These areas of legislation yet to be clarified and put into operation. In addition protection of life forms due to Article 27.3(b) of TRIPS is also being addressed by several countries. The Indian Plant Variety Protection & Farmer's Rights Act 2001 has extended right to new variety and seeds not only breeders but also to Farmers, though not for commercial use. India is also actively participating and is party to many proposal on all the issues at WTO, CBD, WIPO and others.

Negotiation and intervention of India at WTO

The ongoing intervention under the auspies of the WTO TRIPS council regarding Article '7' which states that intellectual property Rights ' should contribute to the promotion of technological innovation and dissemination of technology' not for shake of innovation itself but "to the mutual advantage to producer and user of technological knowledge and in manner conducive to social and economic welfare, and the balanceright and obligation". Thus in TRIPS it is very clear that the IPR regime the purpose is not only to protecting commercial interest of IP holder but it is one of the many tools available to society to achieve technological development, its social and economic welfare and innovation. As Peter Drahos Property rightly said " rights confer authority over resources. When authority is granted to the few over resources on which many depend, the few gain power over the goals of the many. This has consequences for both political and economic freedoms with in a society."

CONCLUSION

The aim of Intellectual Property Rights in world regime to achieve economic, social and technological advancement with new innovation together with sustainable development. It is very unfortunate that some the developed countries would like to use IP to perpetuate their hold on innovation and block development of others . It is therefore essential that flexibilities provided by TRIPS Agreement need to be used by developing countries if they want their societies to benefit from innovations. There is balance that has to be made between the legitimate interest of right holders. As for protection of TK under the existing IPR mechanism. There is need to aware the common people holding valuable indigenous knowledge and holder of TK be involved in decision making process .

REFERENCES

1.   www.wipo.int

2.   Ganguly P. Indian Path Towards TRIPS compliance. World Patent Information. 2003 25:143

3.   www.ipiprlawindia.org

4.   Ganguly P. Intellectual Property Rights- unleasing the knowledge economy, New Delhi, India Tata Mc Graw Hill 2001 ISBN 0-07 463860.

5.   http://en.wikipedia.org/wiki/Intellectual_property.

6.   S. lakshmana Prabu, TNK Suriyaprakash, C.Dinesh Kumar : Intellectual Property Rights and Development in India: Pharma Times Vol44 No 07 2012.

7.   M D Nair: TRIPS, WTO and IPR: Protection of Bioresources and Traditional Knowledge Journal of Intellectual Property Rights Vol. 16 Jan.2011 pp 35-37.

8.   Mathur A. 2003 Who own traditional knowledge ? pg. no 96. Indian council for research on International Economic Relation, New Delhi.

9.   Blakeney, M. Protection of Plant Variety and Farmers' Rights ,24 Eur. Prop. Rev. 9-19.

10.   Peter Drahos and J. Braithwite 2000 Important Feudalism: Who Owns the Knowledge Economy?

Chapter-26

INTELLECTUAL PROPERTY RIGHTS AND ITS ROLE IN BIODIVERSITY CONSERVATION AT LOCAL AND GLOBAL CONSIDERATION

R.K. GARG

Centre of Excellence in Biotechnology, M.P. Council of Science & Technology Vigyan Bhawan, Nehru Nagar, Bhopal-462003 (M.P.), India

Biological diversity is the characteristic of life on earth and it is backbone of sustainable development. Biotechnological and other value adding options provide an opportunity for valorising the biodiversity and associated knowledge systems. Recently intellectual property rights are encouraging commercialization of seed development, protection of new plants and animal varieties, microorganisms and genetically modified organisms. As a consequence, our rich biogenetic diversity is being eroded irreversibly. Local ecological practices construct collective biodiversity flows that care for food security, health care, and ecosystem. An alternative approach will bring a balance in between formal Intellectual Property (IP) system and sustainable aspects of biodiversity. This paper questions the capability of overall intellectual property rights over life to improve the source of income and development of the helpless native.

INTRODUCTION

Intellectual Property Rights (IPR) as the term suggests are meant to be rights to ideas and information, which are used in new inventions or processes. These rights enable the holder to exclude imitators from marketing such inventions or processes for specified period of time in exchange the holder is required to disclose the formula or idea behind the product/process. The effect of IPR is therefore monopoly over commercial exploitation of the idea /information, for a limited period of time. The stated purpose of IPRs is to stimulate innovation, by offering higher monetary returns than the market otherwise might provide (Kothari, 1993).

'Biological Diversity' means the variability among living organisms from all sources and the ecological complexes of which they are part and include diversity within species or between species and of eco-systems. 'Biological resources' means plants, animals and microorganisms or parts thereof, their genetic material and by products with actual or potential use or value but does not include human genetic material (Biod Act, 2002). The advent of new biotechnologies and the capacity to identify and incorporate exotic genetic material into commercial products has forced the pace of change in industry and in Intellectual Property systems. Extensive commercial exploitation of genetic diversity catalyzed by research and development for obtaining IPR will decide the future of our rich biodiversity (Sarr and Swanoson, 2012).

Biological diversity and genetic resources, knowledge and technology play a major role in the relationship between questions of intellectual property and the broad implementation of the Convention of Biological Diversity (CBD). The concerns about global biodiversity, the expansion of intellectual property rights, and the growth of biotechnology are causing conflicts worldwide. Indigenous peoples claim that both their native plants and their knowledge become privatised by biotechnological corporations.

Genetic Resources

Genetic resources have become an issue of high priority to scientists, industry, politicians and even the public at large, for a variety of reasons. Although they form a warehouse of enormous use potentials for plant (Tanksley and Mc Couch, 1997) and animal breeding, in food, chemical and environmental industries, and in pharmaceuticals and medicine (their existence is increasingly endangered. The use of genetic resources and how their benefits are shared in accordance with CBD, one might at first conclude that patents on results of the use of genetic resources, for example new pharmaceutical products, which should ensure benefits, meaning profits, are necessary for creating these benefits and therefore have a supportive function. Moreover, they create incentives to innovate and thus to use genetic resources. On a global basis, human cultural diversity is associated with the remaining concentrations of biodiversity. In fact, evidences exist of remarkable overlaps between global mappings of the world's areas of high biological richness and areas of high diversity of languages, the single best indicator of a distinct culture. The above correlation can be certified both on a country by country basis as well as using biogeographic criteria (Lerch, 1998).

Conserving biodiversity by empowering indigenous peoples

During the past three decades, as the loss of landscapes, habitats, species and genes, has become an issue of international concern, the protected areas of the world have increased notably both in size and number. However, as protected areas expanded, it became evident that the North originated model of uninhabited national parks could not be applied worldwide. Today, there are just nearly 10,000 nationally protected areas (parks and other reserves) in more than 160 countries, covering some 650 million of hectare which represents over 5 percent of earth's land surface (Sedjo and Simpson, 1995).

Many of the areas that have been established as protected areas and many of those that are suitable for future addition to the protected area network are the homelands of indigenous peoples. In Latin America alone, over 80 per cent of protected areas are estimated to have indigenous people living within them. On the other hand, large tracts of the territories under indigenous control, estimated in between 12 and 20 per cent of the earth's surface, are in the scope of conservationists as future reserves (Heywood, 1995). Some authors like Alcorn (1994) think the bulk of the world's biodiversity is embodied within the limits of the indigenous territories of the tropical countries. Given the above, as well as the evidences offered and discussed in the previous sections, the idea that biodiversity conservation is impossible without the participation of indigenous communities is increasingly gaining recognition in national and international conservation circles. For example, in its latest guidelines, IUCN's Commission on National Parks and Protected Areas (1994) consider that indigenously established.

CONCLUSIONS

Biodiversity, biotechnological innovations, and ecological knowledge are increasingly becoming hybrid. The successful development of biological diversity will depend upon creative relationship that can be nurtured between two opposite poles-formal innovative and community systems. The research accumulated in the three last decades by investigators belonging to the fields of conservation biology has evolved convergently towards a shared principle that world's biodiversity only will be effectively preserved by preserving diversity of cultures and vice-versa. This common statement evidences geographical overlap between biological richness and linguistic diversity and between indigenous territories and biologically high-value regions (actual and projected protected areas). Therefore, an alternative biodiversity paradigm that benefits most interests in nature, which maintains contextualized and coevolving biodiversity flows, and that empowers knowledge and life of the poorest people must be urgently explored, not abandoned.

ACKNOWLEDGEMENT

The author wish to thank Prof. Pramod K. Verma, Director General, MPCST & Scientific Advisor to Government of Madhya Pradesh for his moral support all the time and we also wish to thank to Dr. N.K. Choubey, Senior Scientist and In-charge, IPR Division, MPCST, Bhopal assisted during preparation of this review article.

REFERENCES

1.   Alcom, J. (1993). Indigenous peoples and conservation. *Conservation Biology* 7: 424-426.

2.   Biodiversity Act (2002). No.93 of 2002 of Ministry of Environment and Forests, Government of India, New Delhi, India.

3.   Heywood V.H. (ed.) (1995). Global Biodiversity Assessment, Cambridge, UNEP and Cambridge University Press.

4. Kothari A. (1993). Biodiversity and Intellectual Property Rights: Can the two coexist, Journal from *Kalpavriksh-Environment Action Group*, 2: 1-3.

5. Lerch, A. (1998). Property rights and biodiversity. European Journal of Law and Economics, 6: 285-304.

6. Sarr M. and Swanson T. (2012). Intellectual Property and Biodiversity: When and Where are Property Rights Important?. *The Graduate Institute Geneva Centre for International Environmental Studies*, 10: 1-29.

7. Sedjo, R.A. and Simpson, R.D. (1995). 'Property rights, externalities and biodiversity' in Swanson, T.M. (ed.): *The Economics and Ecology of Biodiversity Decline: the Forces Driving Global Change*, Cambridge University Press, pp.79-88.

8. Tanksley and Mc-Couch (1997). Seed Banks and Molecular Maps: Unlocking Genetic Potential from the Wild, 277 Science, 1063.

INDEX

www.ingramcontent.com/pod-product-compliance
Lightning Source LLC
Chambersburg PA
CBHW020753300326
41914CB00050B/180